His Mosaic

From Brokenness to Beauty

Laurie Morris Goddu

Endorsements

"I have had the privilege of knowing Laurie for many years. Her friendship and her story have impacted my life in profound ways. Her's is a story of faith in the midst of suffering, healing and redemption. In this new book, Laurie vulnerably shares her story in a way that inspires hope, faith and increased intimacy with the Lord. I was challenged and inspired."
Stefanie Hinman MS-ATR, BCCC

"I love honest but redemptive stories. Laurie's personal journey in His Mosaic makes us realize how loved we are by are heavenly Father. It's the story of a fractured woman who, through much pain and through the Father's encouragement, became a worshipper/healer. If you listen to a healer you want to make sure they are themselves walking in body, soul and spirit health. She beautifully outlines how, through pain and tragedy "the Father had given me an ability to make people suffering from inner pain feels safe." His Mosaic is a triumph of faith over fear, forgiveness over offense and leaves you with the firm hope...that if God can do it for Laurie, he can do it for me!"
Jon Petersen Author, 24-7 Communities Leader

"Laurie beautifully and courageously shares from her own story with powerful lessons and insights that help us all follow Jesus in a

more whole and courageous way. Her story shows us that God sees us and carries us and he is faithful to fulfill His promises even if they don't look anything like what we imagined. Laurie has given us a gift in this book but her life is a true testament and gift of a 'yes' to Jesus when it's been hard and joyful. Her 'yes' has led her back to the heart of the Father over and over again and it will lead you there too."
Adam & Juli Cox Pastors of Navah Church

"In a transparent and vulnerable narrative, Laurie Goddu opens her heart in the book *His Mosaic*. Readers will be challenged and encouraged by Laurie's spiritual pilgrimage through shame, loss and fear into a world of faith, deliverance and hope. Not only will you be able to identify with her story, but more importantly, she chronicles her journey with resources and insights to light your path. Being a musician by training, Laurie adds prayers and lyrics at the end of each chapter which will prompt you to burst into song. I especially love chapter seven, which is worth the price of the book alone. If you need oil for your lamp, *His Mosaic* will fill you up with a fresh supply, guided by the Holy Spirit, and guaranteed to relight your life and work. I heartily recommend her newest and very readable book."
Ken R. Canfield, PhD. Founder, National Center for Fathering and Grandkids Matter

Dedication

I dedicate this book to:

The Lord for His purposes. He has been my Savior, my Friend, my Comforter, my Teacher, my Father and my Husband. He has rescued me from myself.

My amazing, steadfast, supportive and loving husband Tim, who helped me find the time to see this project to fruition, who endured reading and rereading my story, who is my cheerleader in all things.

My wonderful, forgiving children, Brooke, Heather, Collin and Brynne, who have endured living with me in all the seasons of life and changes I've gone through. Thank you for loving me, being patient with me, and letting me grow and change, while embracing me with my idiosyncrasies!

Acknowledgments

Thank you to my amazing friend and editor, Gloria Cotten, for understanding who I am and helping me write the story clearly. You are an amazing cheerleader for so many women! What a gift!

Sarah Thiessen, who has pioneered in a field where Christians haven't dared to go very often; who brilliantly teaches on the science of the body and theology and has paved a path for healing for many through study and prayer, and impartation.

Mary Andrews, of Mary Andrews Design, who did an amazing job with the cover and depicting the Father's creating something beautiful.

Table of Contents

Foreword

For the past several years, people who have heard me speak or read my first book, *Shattered, and Then...*, have asked me when I was going to write a sequel, as I'd not really finished the story in 2007. I knew I was supposed to write more books, and had prophetic confirmation of this, but I didn't know how to go about it while working full-time and being a single mom.

When the Father sent my new husband, Tim, to me in 2016, I began to look again at how to create space to write. We prayed about the timing and felt that I was to focus the year of 2019 on getting the next book done, plus a few other projects.

As I prayed about what to call this sequel to my first book, *Shattered, and Then...*, I was quickly impressed with His Mosaic, as part of the title. I have called my LLC and ministry His Mosaic for years, so it felt appropriate to describe the Lord's outworking in my journey of restoration this way. Let me give you a little history on how the name, "His Mosaic Ministries" came into being.

During the first few years after my first husband David passed away, I was attending an annual networking and oversight conference sponsored by Jim Hodges and other leaders I'd been relating to for years. Federation of Ministers and Churches International (FMCI is the name of the network that sponsored the conference and was also the network that ordained me)

One night during the conference, Dutch Sheets passed me a hand-written note with a prophetic word on it for me. David and I had been worship pastors in a church led by Dutch, so receiving a prophecy from him was significant to me. He referenced a story from his book,

Tell Your Heart to Beat Again. [1] In the book Dutch recounts the story of an artisan who had been finishing the decor of a palace of a King in Tehran. He had ordered sheets of mirrors, but when they arrived, they were broken. The artisan asked the King not to throw the pieces away but to let him work with them. He had them shattered into millions of pieces. When he was finally finished, it was an incredibly beautiful mosaic! The Father shared with Dutch, "No one will recognize Laurie after I am done with the mosaic I am making from her life."

This word brought hope and made sense to me on so many levels. God has blessed me with several different spiritual gifts and He had used me in a variety of ways to facilitate healing in people's lives. I had no idea how all these different pieces of my personality and character and calling were going to fit together. That note from Dutch gave me, brought a sense of purpose and peace. God Himself was creating something beautiful from the trauma and loss of my life story.

God has used me in speaking and exhortation, teaching and imparting understanding, "psalming" over people with flute and piano and song, and pastoral and prayer counseling. He's brought me keys for unraveling ways that people cope with trauma that are unhealthy, and He has consistently led me toward a non-professional or lay perspective for healing. He is also presently having me do "body work" combined with prayer and submitted to the Holy Spirit. More on that later...all for His glory. The gifts and the understanding all come from "the Father of Lights... in whom there is no shadow!" [2]

The prophetic word from Dutch was not only the core for the ministry that the Lord had me start, but it is also the way I approach working with people. I'm continually asking myself (and Jesus), "What tool in the toolbox is the one that will turn the key and unlock this person's healing?" I don't believe there is any one tool that works for

---

[1] Dutch Sheets, *Tell Your Heart to Beat Again* (Ventura: Regal House Publishing, 2002).
[2] *Amplified Holy Bible*, James 1:17 ((Nashville: Zondervan Publishing House and The Lockman Foundation, 2015).

everyone all the time. God always wants us looking to Him for help and guidance and wisdom. His Holy Spirit is the revelator and healer, so there's no one better to partner with!

As you read the rest of my story, I trust the Holy Spirit will individualize what I share for your own life journey. I trust He will give what you, personally, need: whether you need comfort and healing, or a change of perspective, or different language to connect the dots in order to see how the Father has been leading you, healing you, aligning you with His truth. God will give you what you need!

You will notice that I often talk about God speaking to me, or talking to me. I want to emphasize that when I say this I usually mean I've sensed Him, or had an impression, or had a strong feeling in my gut, not that I have heard an audible voice. Sometimes I've heard a tiny whisper with words. Sometimes I've been reading something and a phrase jumps out. Sometimes I've had a dream, or seen a picture in my mind. Sometimes the Scripture has "spoken" to me. Sometimes I've sensed in my gut a direction from Him. God speaks in such a myriad of ways. He communicates emotionally, physically, and through our senses; He imparts His peace and reminds us of Scriptures; He speaks direction to our spirit. All of these ways and more I identify as His speaking to, or leading us.

Please don't be intimidated by this language; it's only my way of communicating my experience. Often clients share with me that they don't believe they hear God, yet when I begin working with them, they suddenly realize that they hear Him clearly, but have discounted their hearing! My journey has honed my hearing Him. I hope that my sharing these experiences will encourage you in your faith journey as well as confirm ways God has spoken to you that you may not recognize.

When I'm unsure of the way or don't understand what's going on, focusing on the Lamb in worship is the way I settle myself. I'm a worshipper first and foremost. This song came to me as I was waiting before the Lord and praying at the Sheets' home in Colorado Springs in a time of transition when I was asking the Father for direction for my future, back in the early 2000's.

Worthy is the Lamb
Holy is His name
Righteous and just, forever the same
Worthy is the Lamb
Glory to His name
Faithful and true, forever You remain

Jesus so worthy, No other so holy
Jesus the Lamb that was slain

Your precious blood cleanses our souls
Freeing us from our sin
All glory and honor are Yours
Who sits upon the Throne

The King of Kings and Lord of Lords
The majesty of Heav'n adored

Jesus so worthy, No other so holy
Jesus the Lamb that was slain
Laurie Morris ©

Unto You be all the glory, To You be all the praise
Laurie Prophet Morris Goddu
www.hismosaic.com

Chapter 1: My Abrahamic Journey

Have you ever had God direct you to do something that made no natural sense or something that went against normal counsel and wisdom? I have had such experiences throughout my walk with Jesus, and when it has involved a change of location or direction, I've referred to it as an Abrahamic journey. No, I'm not equating myself with one of the fathers of the faith! However, God the Father led Abraham to do things that made no sense practically, or that had no clear goal in sight, and Abraham followed God. I want to do the same!

I've also been told through prophecy that I'm a Jeremiah, one who sees with pictures, and my life has often displayed a parallel to what God is saying in the moment. Sometimes my circumstances foretell the future or give wisdom about things God is addressing in the Church. I didn't have to make this happen; God made this happen.

Let's back up a bit for a quick overview of my early adult life before I jump into the later leading of the Lord and my faith journey.

I was married to the late David Morris, a well-known worship leader, songwriter and author. We had overcome much in our marriage, including David's infidelity with men, and his healing from a personality disorder, Dissociative Identity Disorder (also known in the

'90's as Multiple Personality Disorder). We had finally both become healthy in our marriage and were enjoying each other and life when, in 2002, he was diagnosed with stage four lung cancer. He passed away after a short but intense four and a half month battle.

We had been worship pastors at a wonderful church in North Carolina. However, several months after his passing, I felt sure I couldn't grieve appropriately there. The church body we had been a part of didn't have the capacity for what my family and I needed at that time, i.e. lots of personal fathering and close oversight. In addition, David had been so well loved that the worship team was having trouble letting him go and embracing the new worship pastor. My continued presence was only making that issue more difficult.

Our church was a transient community in a military town, deeply influenced by the military's "every man for himself" mindset. Intimate relationships were not their focus, but my children and I needed intimate emotional support. In addition, I felt the weight of real or imagined expectations from the people that I should be okay. So I began asking the Lord if I could or should relocate in order to heal.

I knew that I should not make such a big decision the first year. I had lived through a sudden, abrupt move as a young girl after my father died. This early experience gave me the foresight to include my four kids in my decision-making process so that they did not experience the same level of challenges I faced with such an emotion-packed decision. Three of my children were teens at the time and the youngest was nine. They were not certain at all about moving, but respected my leading from the Lord. I had three places that I felt led to consider and pray about. None of the places had deep past relational connection, but they were what I felt the Holy Spirit was highlighting.

After months of praying, getting counsel, and talking with my kids, the Lord whispered a specific word to my heart. He said that the place where He would take our family would have my son's name written on it. I had no idea what this meant, but I wasn't thinking it meant literally! However, a visit to Collinsville, Illinois, made it clear that this was the place --- my son's name is Collin. On that trip, God made it clear that He was taking us to this "oasis" to heal.

There were additional details that confirmed our move to Collinsville, one of which just made me smile. The house God provided for us was located on Chapel Drive, in Morris Heights, of all things! What a fun sign from the Father for the Morris family! The church there gave us the intimate, loving support we needed as we grieved and healed and found a new normal without David.

Although Gideon asked for signs, I consider signs to be the "icing on the cake" or the extra kiss from the Father once He has given direction. In my experience with the prophetic, giving and receiving words from God, I have found that waiting with open hands is a safe way to see if there is confirmation and assurance that it is God Who is speaking. For example, when I'm considering if a thought is really from the Lord, I wait until circumstances change, or doors open, or there are encouragements or ideas from people who don't know what's going on in my life that support or contradict what I'm sensing. I'll give you more specifics later on this.

After our move to Collinsville, God also fulfilled His promise to bring us a family that would walk with us through our grieving. This gift was very important to me because, when David was alive, we had committed to a few single women to walk alongside and support them in their journeys. We went to court with them, helped school some of their kids, and cried and prayed with them in difficulties. One of those moms is still in relationship with me to this day. So I asked the Lord to bring recompense for this and He did! God gave us a precious younger couple and their extended family to support us through the pain of that season of grief. There were two other families that surrounded us during that time as well, and I am forever grateful and forever changed by their love. They encouraged and challenged and included us in their lives with open arms. What a gift they were! The Galloways are still amazing friends and "family" today. What an incredible God we serve! He knows our needs, and He has given us the blessing of reaping what we sow if we partner with Him.

3

The three years I was living in Collinsville were both challenging and wonderful. The church body there cared and watched over my children and me very lovingly. However, I was grieving and trying to find a sense of direction for my life. I was processing what my new identity and purpose in life was without David. None of my friends could direct me or make this process shorter. No one was asking me to lead worship or to speak on it, and these activities had been mostly what I did with David. We had traveled the world together, leading scores of people into the throne room of God and teaching on a lifestyle of worship. Now here I was, directionless and grieving,

While I was not working full-time, I was revisiting old areas of pain and betrayal and working through forgiveness towards myself, David and God at a deeper level. The slowed down schedule and the "new normal" were allowing me to look at things I hadn't been able to process fully when life had been at full steam ahead.

Many people have described our emotions as like an onion being peeled, layer by layer, and creating tears. During my time in Collinsville, God was peeling off more layers of old pain that I thought were completely resolved. God stretched me in so many areas! He redefined my desires and redirected my focus with each new job. It is kind of funny to look back on, but I ended up being a counselor to my co-workers everywhere I worked. God was helping me see who He'd made me to be. Though I had lost my career and, seemingly, my calling along with David, God was helping me find who I was and what I was supposed to do with the rest of my life.

Learning to process the pain through my personal worship became a new normal in this season. I had never written music before (except a few lines of a song, and only with David), but now I was writing new songs regularly as a part of my personal devotional life. Melodies and words kept coming to me so I wrote them down in childlike scribble as I did not know how to notate chords. In addition to the counseling, God was adding songwriting to my new direction. I honestly thought God was silent during this season, until a year later when I realized that He had been "talking" to me through my musical expressions!

4

During those months of songwriting, I kept having the impression that I should record a CD. This idea made no sense to me as I knew that my piano playing and songwriting were not on a par with others musical gifts. There were plenty of people out there who were amazing! An internal argument arose in me every time I felt the impression to follow through on the idea of making a CD, so I kept waiting, and kept writing.

Do you know that our obedience partnered with faith opens doors? A dear friend of mine from Bible school added her faith to mine when she heard some of the songs I had written. Char and her husband believed with me for God to bring into my life the people who would help me produce the CD. Several years of prayer followed before she was able to introduce me to an amazing couple in Nashville. There was a divine connection from the start with the Wethey's. They joined us in faith and prayer, adding their own creativity and talent. Bruce arranged the music I had written and my CD began to take shape. It was a faith journey all the way, jump started by Char and Kirk's generosity of giving and faith in the project.

I knew the CD was a Psalms project. Like David, the psalmist of the Bible, I was pouring out my heart to God during a time of grief and healing. There were songs of lament and songs of hope. The production and arrangements were also faith projects: though it didn't make rational sense to me to make a CD, I trusted God and followed Him through the open doors as they presented themselves. I ended up producing the CD shortly after my first book came out. The project is called *Restore Me*. The final production is a collection of instrumental and vocal pieces intended to minister to those going through difficult seasons of change in their lives. It was such an integral part of my own healing as I expressed sorrow and the different stages of grief through the music.

Obedience is always worth it! I haven't made much money off the proceeds of *Restore Me* as I've given most of my copies away, but that music has ministered to many and I have been blessed to hear some of their stories. Best of all, I can stand before the Father confident that I obeyed and used the gift He released in me.

By the time my daughter and her husband encouraged me to return to North Carolina to live in 2006, focused grieving was at a close and I was ready to leave Collinsville. We moved back to Fayetteville, NC, where God began to challenge me to quit my job and to write the story of David's and my struggles and eventual victory in our marriage. I had never even considered writing a book until the Father gave me a prophetic exhortation through someone that I was going to write books. My pastor and others I respected strongly confirmed that this leading was from God: it was time for our story to be told. Others needed to hear of the hope and healing that David and I had obtained from our bumpy, broken journey together.

Writing *Shattered, and Then…* provided another time of processing for me. I found my voice with writing, and was able to honor God for what He had done in my own heart and for what He had done in David and me as a couple. The book became a tool for God to use to build His Kingdom, but He also used the process of writing to bring deeper healing to me from the trauma of the journey in my marriage. It was important for me to release what God had been teaching me and to bring hope to others in hard places. I titled the book as I did because of the beauty of the restoration and comfort that God brought in our marriage, and in my life through the struggles.

Timing, in the Father's directives, is so important! Sometimes obedience is needed immediately and other times there are years of waiting in faith until the right moment. Listening and waiting in dependence upon the Holy Spirit are both important to learn, as they strengthen our relationship and trust in Him.

Sometime in that first year back in North Carolina, God gave me a dream. I didn't initially think the dream was from Him because it was so short and direct. I had already decided to ignore it when the Lord let me know that He had sent it to me. The morning after the dream, a friend and mentor of mine showed up at my house to pray and visit. During our conversation she said, "I think you are supposed to start and lead healing teams here." I about fell over because in the dream I'd gone to my pastor and told him I had a healing protocol that I could put into place at our church. The word protocol was not even a word I used!

Training and leading healing teams was clearly not my idea but God's, so I submitted the idea to my pastor even though I was not confident that he would support the idea. However, he and the elders of our fellowship embraced the plan and released me to create and train teams in the church that would minister emotional healing. As I prayed about the way to train those teams, God brought me into contact with the leaders of Restoring the Foundations (RTF). Out of that connection, and with the support of my pastor and leaders, I embarked on a training program with RTF that lasted over the next few years.

Coming under the constraint of the systematic program of RTF after flowing freely with Holy Spirit all the years of my previous pastoral counseling was challenging, but it was also a great stretching and growing experience. RTF training gave me safe, effective boundaries to work within as I met with individuals for God's perspective on their pain. It was an easy tool for training others as well, more so than some of the other healing approaches I'd studied. I was thankful and relieved that I didn't have to reinvent the wheel and write my own program.

During my training time with RTF, I realized that God was calling me to work full-time in ministry once again, only this time I was to minister in prayer counseling and emotional healing, not music. Isn't it hilarious how we can be doing something and not recognize that it is the thing we are supposed to focus on? I had always ministered in the area of worship and it took several years before I could see what was right in front of me --- counseling and personal ministry were a part of me, and God was calling me to focus there. Since David had died, I'd been questioning my calling. What would my life look like without David and his gifts and leading worship? Now I knew that God still had a purpose for my life with my focus now on personal ministry instead of worship.

Over the next several years I founded and led the HEAL ministry for Manna Church. I trained teams there to do what my ministry partner and I were doing with people one on one. I grew in my ability to follow the Holy Spirit's leading to bring healing in people's hearts and minds. Daily I was dependent on His specific leading to help hurting people receive His healing and perspective. It was a confidence-building time as I learned to listen to Him and as I saw Him move supernaturally in the lives of people. I worked in a team of two during those years, and found that it strengthened my hearing the Holy Spirit, as my ministry partner Rebecca and I would often hear the same things!

If you are unsure of God's voice, practice, practice! Keep asking questions and don't be afraid to ask God for specific confirmations. I believe the Lord loves to use pictures and stories to illustrate what He is teaching us, just as He did in the New Testament with parables. He likes to keep us engaged with Him and often answers our questions in ways that keep us asking questions. He enjoys our relationship with Him so He keeps us in conversation and keeps us digging in the Scriptures for Truth. When you don't understand something, keep asking for clarification from the Holy Spirit until you have what you need. If it's God talking, the words will align with the Bible, His nature, and His principles.

During the years of living back in North Carolina, besides training and writing my book, I was privileged to travel with teams to South Africa and Sri Lanka, to teach on healing and to impart some of what God had taught me in my walk with the Lord. These trips strengthened my confidence in what God wanted me to deposit in others about worship and emotional healing. Just as in my twenties and thirties, traveling to other nations had affected me much more than it had impacted the people I was ministering to. Those trips were always more about furthering my own training and preparation than it was about helping the people I ministered to. God's exposure of so many cultures introduced me to many different paradigms for worshipping and serving God. I learned that we Americans don't have the corner on the market on anything!

About the middle of 2010, while still running healing teams in Fayetteville for Manna Church, I began hearing God say the word, "shift," in prayer. The more I prayed about it, the bigger and louder the word felt. I also heard God say, "transition". I sensed God was speaking to me personally, but that He was also speaking about something that was happening all across the Body of Christ. I was not thinking that this meant moving anywhere. My youngest daughter Brynne was entering her junior year of high school and I was enjoying living near my daughter Heather, son-in-law Jon, and my grandkids.

Simultaneously with hearing these words, I began recognizing that I felt isolated in my church community. God had given me a gift of leadership yet I was not officially in leadership in the church. I was a contract consultant. It felt very awkward and I didn't know where I fit in. I was also physically exhausted. I shared these issues with a few close friends, asking them to pray for healing or for a new deposit of grace. My body was "talking" or displaying my stress level and I began having symptoms that indicated trouble. Then I had a dream that brought clarity on the reality of my emotional and physical overload. I was so grateful to God for speaking to me this way.

In the dream I was in my house and two people that represented Jesus and the Holy Spirit were there. Jesus said that my furnace was running constantly on emergency heat and it was a miracle that it hadn't failed. He also pointed out that the back door of my home was unlocked and vulnerable. This picture confirmed to me that, like the furnace, I was close to physical burn-out, not a good place for anyone, but especially not for someone who is helping others process trauma. Concurrently, I was experiencing a growing longing to spend more time with the Lord in worship, a longing to write more, and a desire for a smaller, more close-knit community. As a single mom working full-time, I was feeling the lack of intimate friendships with others outside of clients.

Dream Wow!

9

Several months later, I felt impressed to attend a conference at my alma mater, Christ for the Nations Institute in Dallas, Texas. I had not visited there in many years, so the leading to return felt significant. My former pastor Dutch Sheets was speaking at the conference about a shift that he saw coming. He shared a message on David moving his household to devote himself to worship and prayer. I felt such a strong presence of the Lord on this message and something leapt in me. I immediately began thinking about my longings for different rhythms and for possibly moving. Once more I began to wonder if the Lord was leading me in a new direction.

There were several other areas of discomfort in my life other than its pace. By this time in my journey I had learned that running from pressures or conflicts is not wisdom. The Lord wants us to resolve things, not escape from them! The tension produced by not running from the pressures of life, creates a potential for growth and for greater intimacy with Him and others. I resolved to wait on the Lord until it was clear that He was leading me in a different direction or to a new place. As is often the case, when we let go of something we've held onto, God will move because we are letting Him be God.

By January of 2011 the word "SHIFT" was ringing loudly and daily in my head. I had been voicing this growing sense to my close friends and they were praying for me. After meditating on that conference message from Dutch Sheets, I knew the shift was for me personally but that it also had to do with the church corporately, but I did not know what to do about it. One night as I cried out to the Lord intensely, asking whether I was to leave or stay in Fayetteville, I sang out these words while playing my piano:

> **In the middle of confusion and my fear**
> **In the middle of my questions I look up and draw near**
> **In the middle of my anger and my shame**
> **In the middle of failures I look up and call Your name**
> **In the middle of my loneliness and my grief**
> **In the middle of the silence I look up and You speak.**

Then He began to sing a song back to me:

Let go child
Let go and trust me
I am here, waiting to catch you, waiting to show you the way.
So let go and give it up child, let go and give it all up to Me
I am Your Father, I'm faithful

And I responded to Him:

I let go, I let go of my fear, I let go of my doubt, I let
go...falling into Your arms, my place of safety and rest, into Your
loving arms I rest.

Laurie M Goddu ©

Peace flooded me and weeping overwhelmed me, as I took a deep breath and received what He was saying to me.

The next morning, I randomly checked Facebook, and a man I didn't know had posted a prophetic word to me. My heart began to pound as I read the words, "A rising tide of opportunities are coming your way, but the decision you will be compelled to make is based on the drawing to intimacy with Me. The stream you will enter will make your heart glad and the hearts of those you are with. Don't be pushed – be led." As I read the words several times through, I knew in my heart that I was leaving Fayetteville and the ministry I'd been leading.

Even with this profoundly confirming prophetic word, I still wanted more confirmation. I was 51 years old and thinking of moving somewhere with no job or specific purpose other than to take a sabbatical. I needed to be sure! After asking the Father for more confirmation, He brought it in several wonderful and surprising ways with people approaching me with confirming scriptures and impressions over the ensuing months.

I want to interject here that it is so important not to just follow signs and prophetic words but to weigh in prayer the Lord's directive! As I shared in the foreword, prophetic words and confirming signs are often the "icing on the cake". I believe that when you hear something from God directly, you should put it in the invisible, simmering pot behind you and see what's left of it in a few weeks or months. Bounce things off others who pray for you, and wait for the Father's specific confirmation from the Scripture. Pay attention to those who operate in the prophetic, but also to the opening of doors. It is so important to have assurance in your heart to stabilize you when others hear different things. I've seen people follow purported "prophetic words" when there was no confirmation, and their lives were derailed. They ended up with devastated hearts, blaming God for not fulfilling what they had been told. We must weigh and discern prophetic things, no matter who the word comes through! When I eventually shared with others that God was leading me to move, there were several people who "prophesied" where I was moving, but they were wrong. Their predictions were not where I ended up. The reality that we are broken human vessels applies to us all. The Holy Spirit is choosing to use these vessels to deliver His hope and heart, but we are not always filtering it all correctly. All of us perceive things and share things that may not be fully accurate.

When I shared with an intercessor friend of mine about my possible transition, she invited me to come to her home to pray and wait on the Lord for more specifics about where I was moving. While on the flight to her home, the Lord asked me if I was willing for my time of prayer away to be different from what I expected. I had no idea what that meant, but said yes in my heart.

Over the next few days at Kim's home, while journaling and praying, I kept seeing the letters IHOP in my minds eye. I was familiar with the International House of Prayer in Kansas City, as my son Collin had gone to school there. He had been asking me for over a year to consider moving there, but I'd thought he was crazy! I didn't feel drawn to be involved in this ministry so I was unsure what the Lord meant by showing me this.

Then Kim invited me to go with her to hear Jane Hamon speak at her church. Initially, I didn't want to go, since my focus was to wait on the Lord, but when I asked, Jesus said to me, "I have something for you there." When I told Kim that I would go with her, she confessed that she had had a vision of Jane Hamon pointing to me and calling me out by name to prophesy over in the meeting. Kim did not know that Jane had prophesied over me before, a strategic word as I was leaving Collinsville to return to North Carolina. God's speaking to Kim made me realize that He was arranging things in ways I could never have foreseen. At the meeting that night, after closing the service in prayer, Jane turned and called out to me to come forward, just as my friend had said! Jane prophesied that I was in a season of shift and revelation. (There was that word again!) However, even with all this prophetic confirmation, I still didn't know any of the practicalities, like how I was going to make a living or where I was to live.

Interestingly, when I returned home I heard about a possible job opening in IHOP's counseling department. I took heart that there might really be a place for me in Kansas City. Sometimes God uses a "hook" to pull us towards where we are to go, and this was my hook to "hang" my faith on.

Since by now, I'd had numerous confirmations, I took courage and started planning for a move. There were three people I knew living in Kansas City at the time, so I wrote them about housing. One of them, an old friend from Dallas, offered a one room apartment over a garage to Brynne and me at a rate I could afford. However, I was still struggling with some fear. There were still unanswered questions that were important. One of the biggest was the question of whether Brynne would be going with me or would stay back in North Carolina with my one of my other daughters. I had given her the option of staying with her sister Brooke and her husband Branden, or of going with me. I wanted her to have a choice in the matter. Over several months, she received words of encouragement that led her to choose going with me. I was overjoyed! Neither of us realized that saying yes to moving would mean sharing a bed for a year. Yowser! Often in following the Lord's directive we don't know what it's really going to be like. But we were committed to the move now and making plans with strong intention.

Even with all the confirmations, there were a few folks who didn't support my decision to move because my house in Fayetteville had not sold.

So I went back to the Lord to ask once again for more confirmation. I was certain God was directing me to move, but I needed to be sure the time was now. God came through once again! Another word, through a prophet in our network, brought me the assurance that I was to move forward as planned. The word was about my plowing in the fields of the Midwest and moving into areas of my specialty. It also indicated that I would be reconnecting with old relationships, not just making new ones. Both of these things happened as the result of my move.

We said tearful goodbyes to family and friends, but we were also excited about what the move was going to bring. As we settled into our little one-room home in south Kansas City, I began my six weeks of sabbatical. Unsure of what the next step was, I buckled down in prayer, waiting for direction of my next steps. Remember the possible counseling position at IHOP? Well, I knocked on that door but it was clearly not for me, so I said no. It served its purpose of momentary encouragement but it was not the place God had for me. It was what I said earlier, only a hook to hang my faith on.

Several weeks into my sabbatical, a knock came at the door. There was a woman on my doorstep with my book, *Shattered, and Then...,* in her hand. She introduced herself and shared that Brynne had given her my book when she first met her. She jumped straight to the reason for her visit. "Would you meet with me and my husband and help us work through his infidelity?" I was taken by surprise. At that point I had no intention of counseling or doing personal ministry. I prayed about her request, knowing that I would have to come up with a grid to use with them that was different from what I'd been doing the past several years. Within days, God was answering my prayers and assuring my heart. I said yes to them, and so began working with marriages and families in Kansas City. This initial connection led to another and another over the next year. That was in the fall of 2011 and I've been seeing folks full-time ever since with many restored hearts!

When the Father gives you a door or opportunity, OBEY! His leadership is impeccable even though it doesn't always make rational sense.

I am not licensed, nor do I have a degree in counseling (although I am ordained and function under a pastoral covering for counseling), yet I have seen thousands of people through the past twenty five-plus years walk into healing and freedom through the Holy Spirit working through me. Partnering with the Holy Spirit at all times is the key to our success in all we do!

Over the next year it became apparent that Brynne and I needed our own space. I had started teaching some small classes on healing and was seeing clients in my landlord's home. Using someone else's house was getting awkward, so we began asking the Lord for another place to live. He answered beautifully through a family we knew. They invited us to live in a basement apartment in their new home.

Have you ever given an answer to something without fully praying or processing about it? Well that's what I did here. I immediately said no to my friend's offer out of fear of offending my landlord. The timing of the offer was short of the year's commitment I'd made to her. When we respond to fear it usually doesn't end up well, but God had a new lesson for me to learn. Did you know that Jesus is a God Who redeems even our mistakes? Yes, He gives us second chances!

I waited a few days, shedding many tears before the Lord, before I asked my landlord to release me from my commitment to our garage apartment. Then I gave my friends a call to see if their basement apartment was still available. She informed me sadly that another single mom had taken the apartment. I was so bummed and again cried. However, I felt the Lord's prompting to ask Him for the space back, in faith. This felt a bit crazy and selfish, but I prayed, "Lord, if this home was Your intended spot for us, then bring it back, or bring something better!"

About two weeks later, I received a call from my friend Laura, saying that the other single mom wouldn't be renting the space after all. I was overjoyed! The next days were crazy as I made plans to fly to North Carolina, retrieve my furniture from storage, and drive back to Kansas City with my possessions in a UHaul truck! What a trip that was, driving that big 24-foot truck with my life in the back. God graciously sent a friend to drive with me on that long trip in that big, bouncing truck, so it actually felt like more of an adventure than a chore. I was closing the door completely to North Carolina and beginning to truly plant in Kansas City.

Brynne and I lived with Laura and her husband and their son Malachi, for almost four years. Living with that family gave us a home that was peaceful and protected, and Brynne and I finally had separate bedrooms. They received us into their home gladly, and Laura became a steady source of referrals for my counseling business. I believe she's got a reward in heaven for the people she sent to me that were healed and restored!

Just as we settled into new rhythms of home, I began settling into a local church as well, helping to support through teaching on healing with dear friends, from my Bible school days. About two years later the Lord led me to the fellowship I'm still a part of today. This church is the place God told me about through the prophet on Facebook, "a different stream," and one where I feel intimately connected to the Father and to the community.

Father God, would you remind me of the way You have led me into paths of righteousness? Would you help me remember the miracles of Your provision and leading? Would you help me give thanks for every directive You have brought that has caused me to know You more and depend upon You more? Give me courage to obey the things that don't always make sense. Thank You for

Your will in me and for equipping me for what You have called me to. Thank you for being a good shepherd and leading me to still waters to restore my soul. Thank you for all the places You have redeemed.

You have gone before and You will guard behind
Scattering the fear and exposing every lie
Call us out by name and lead us by Your light
We follow You, we follow You

You're a sweet, sweet Shepherd
What a treasure to be found in You
You're a good, good Shepherd
It's our honor to follow You

Voice like many waters with fire in Your eye
Searching through the earth for broken hearts to find
Every heart Your portion and every home Your prize
We follow You, we follow You

You seek the lost, You bring back the stray
You bind up the broken-hearted and give the weak Your strength
You will have Your bride, Your inheritance
Praise erupt in every nation, with one voice we sing
We follow You, we follow You, we follow You

©Cutter Gage, 2019, Navah Music

(This song was written by my friend Cutter during our fellowship's journey, (Navah) of following the cloud of the Lord nomadically throughout Kansas City.)

Chapter 2: His Sovereign Thread Weaving Continuity

Oh the wonder of the sovereignty of God! I am not proposing a theological debate here. I've been consistently challenged by God on the issue of sovereignty for years. I define myself theologically as a "Calmene," someone who believes in both Arminianism and Calvinism. I believe simultaneously in the sovereignty of God and in the part we play in changing God's plans through prayer. I believe our acts of obedience and our intercession affect God's decisions. For me, both beliefs exist together in the scriptures. The longer I have walked with Jesus, and that's currently over 45 years, the less I'm certain of His ways. However, I'm now more certain of Who He is and His heart and character. He is altogether good! Many times people declare that God is sovereign and what they mean is that He can do anything. I like to change up the language and say, there are some things God cannot do --- He cannot lie; He cannot be unfaithful! When I moved to Kansas City, God's goodness was demonstrated over and over to me, not just through my story with God's provision, but in multiple other areas.

When I first planned to go to college and pursue a degree, I wanted to be a music therapist. I recognized, even back then, that music could heal minds and bodies and accomplish something words and medicine could not touch. However, I ended up going to Oral Roberts University, at the Father's clear directive, but they didn't offer a music therapy degree. While attending ORU, I was assigned to do a paper for a class and decided to write on the influence of vibrations on the body, citing Pavlov's experiments with mice, and rock music's effects on inhibitions. I never dreamed that God had a part in my writing that paper. I did not foresee that studying the science of frequencies and their effect on the body would become a part of my future. But God was weaving His thread of direction and calling even then. He held my destiny in His hand and directed my steps in ways I could not have laid out for myself.

Following ORU, I attended Christ for the Nations Institute (CFNI) and encountered the Lord in some new and different ways with different manifestations. One of those ways was feeling His power in my body with a vibrating sensation in my muscles and limbs when others would lay hands on me and pray. I was not in control of this vibration or shaking; it was the power of God manifesting in my physical body. It was a new and unique experience that would eventually prove to be related to understanding more of God's power through vibrational frequencies.

I also had a supernatural experience while ministering at Mardi Gras and witnessing on the streets with a team from CFNI. Our team leader Michael had asked me to bring my flute to use during our corporate prayer times. I told him I didn't play by ear, but only read music. He persisted with his request, so I brought my flute on the trip. One day during corporate intercession, he pointed to me and said, "Prophesy on your flute!" I didn't understand exactly what that meant, and was terrified of what would happen if I played. However, as I picked up my flute and began to blow, there was a wave of weeping that swept from one side of the room to the other and we all began travailing over the lost. Not only did something happen through the music, the sound, and the vibrations of His melody, but I could play by ear perfectly from that moment! Only God can do such a thing. *Yes!*

That trip to New Orleans had a deep impact on my life. One evening as we walked down the streets singing about the blood of Jesus, the massive crowds went silent and parted before us. Other people ran to us, asking how they could be saved. The police later reported to us that there had been no crimes committed in the area where we were singing that evening. No crimes on Bourbon Street during Mardi Gras? That's a miracle! The power of worship and sound and God's frequencies through our song plus the declaration of the power of His blood sacrifice changed the atmosphere.

During the 1990's David and I were pastoring in Colorado Springs and were traveling and teaching on worship around the nation and the world. We taught on chords and keys and what they communicate to our emotions and bodies. We had experienced that music can create peace or discord. We were teaching on something we didn't fully understand, yet this teaching was to lead to a revelation in my future. During this same time, God was giving us one prophetic word after another about a new sound of heaven that would be coming to earth. We didn't know what it meant, but agreed with and cried out for it for several years. The inference was that the sound or frequency of earth (the earth vibrates with a measurable frequency or Hertz) would align with the frequency of heaven, which would release miracles or breakthroughs because of this alignment.

We have all heard stories of healing occurring spontaneously during worship. No one prayed specifically for the hurting person but God healed them as people were worshiping. I believe that the synergy of faith with the vibrations of music brings a release of God's power, and alignment with Heaven. Remember that God spoke the world into existence. The vibrations of sound created by the mouth of God actually brought forth all that is. I believe there is a correlation between vibrations of sound and the release of God's power through His voice.

During that decade, we visited Brownsville Assembly of God with our pastoral team where revival was happening. I was changed forever by seeing God deliver many people from addictions and brokenness, but even more impactful for me was hearing physically, the sound of God's power. As I would approach the front pews of the church, I would begin to hear and feel deep, pulsating vibrations that I have never experienced before or since. The sound of a deep bass vibrating on powerful sound speakers is the only thing close to what I heard and felt. As I would draw nearer to the sound I would cross an invisible line into the front of the sanctuary, and immediately be overcome by the Holy Spirit with shaking. Then I would fall down under God's power. Some call this being "slain" by the Holy Spirit. I did not connect this experience to what God had been showing me about His voice at creation until later. At those meetings in Brownsville, however, I realized that the presence of God was sometimes accompanied by literal vibrations of power.

Some time later, back at home in Colorado Springs in a Sunday morning worship service, God gave me a prophetic word, "I want habitation, not visitation!". As I stood on the platform and spoke forth those words, there was a loud bang at the back of the sanctuary and both power and sound went out on our sound system. I can't prove it, but I'm convinced that the force of the prophetic word and the resonance of my voice agreeing with God in that moment blew out the sound system.

During the 1990's, while traveling with Cindy Jacobs and leading worship for her Glory Fire Conferences, another event involving sound occurred. A young Asian woman, enslaved by demons, had been prayed over for several hours, yet she was not experiencing freedom from her oppression. A friend approached me and told me I needed to sing over her. I was initially hesitant, but my friend insisted that I was supposed to do this. The Holy Spirit had me sing a lullaby over her. As I softly sang the song the Lord had given me for my own children, the demons left and she relaxed into a peaceful sleep.

I didn't understand what happened at the time, but later it made complete sense, as I learned more about the science of energy. God's vibration, or energy, or His Life Force or Ruach, and His frequencies, were delivered through the notes and melody of the music as I sang. In addition, the words that proclaimed Jesus was holding her close and keeping her safe, ministered to an injured place in her soul. Satan had been taking advantage of some trauma in her life to enslave her. The devil is an expert at using painful experiences to gain a foothold in our lives. He is also an expert at using music to influence us. He was created an angel of light, gifted to lead worship in heaven. No wonder Satan has had the influence he has had with all the sounds and frequencies that are in him. No wonder God has called us to worship Him both corporately and privately! Worship is about honor and adoration of Who God is. Deliverance and healing are manifested here on earth because of Who He is in His power, which is also vibrational energy!

There are some who have studied the different frequencies and even musical chords and have taught that to align with God's heavenly sound one must play in a certain key or have a certain frequency operating.[3] I've come to the conclusion that this theory is not a completely accurate belief, since God is outside of time and space. The Scripture says: "The Son is the radiance of God's glory and the exact representation of His nature, upholding all things by His powerful word." [4] "God created all things on the earth, beneath the earth and in the heavens above, yet He exists above and is independent from them. All things are upheld by His mighty power, yet He is upheld by Himself alone." "For from Him, through Him and to Him are all things".[5] As the creator of all energy and life, He is not limited by a particular frequency or sound; He is over it all and in it all. Even so, I do see a correlation between our receptivity to Him and certain frequencies. I do believe we can sometimes feel a connection to God that is tangibly different when certain sounds are being played or sung. However, we don't want to limit our Creator to just one or a few sounds!

---

[3] Michael Tyrell, www.WholeTones.com.
[4] *Berean Study Bible*, Hebrews 1:3a, www.BibleHub.com.
[5] *Berean Study Bible*, Romans 11:36.

God has continued to call me to play prophetically and to sing over others, often with those listening experiencing a profound connection to Him, having visions of Him, or receiving healing of their emotions and mindsets. God's "sound" transcends space and time and goes to the core of people's bodies and souls to bring healing. My late husband used to say, "Music is a spiritual force before it's an audible sound." What I've witnessed proves this to be an accurate statement. The power of music is frequencies that bypass the mind and directly impact the emotions, body and spirit.

While living in Colorado Springs, God also began showing me that our bodies can be healed through touch. I was very much affected for the good by regular massage, so much so that massage therapy became a consistent source of emotional and physical healing for me. During a few of my massage sessions, I experienced a spontaneous release of emotions that clearly were related to past hurts. My massage therapist, and also some of her clients, told me of experiencing a similar release through massage and prayer. During the years after David passed, massage was actually my "safe touch" that helped keep me stabilized and in touch with my emotions. Since our physical bodies and our emotions are connected, it stands to reason that receiving a healing touch in our bodies can produce emotional healing as well. Science and the Bible agree on this principle. Several verses in Proverbs portray emotions as affecting the body for good or bad, for health or sickness. Science has also come to see a correlation between emotions and health. Dr. Don Colbert's book *Deadly Emotions*[6] highlights the mind-body-spirit connection that can heal or destroy you.

God's overlapping threads continued to weave together the mosaic of my life and calling as I was introduced to muscle testing (kinesiology) and to the Rife machine (using frequencies for healing of disease) through Christian chiropractors. I was initially reticent about these methods because I didn't understand the science behind it, and was cautious about things that felt New Age. However, a child for

---

[6] Don Colbert, *Deadly Emotions* (Nashville: Thomas Nelson Books, 2003).

24

whom I babysat was seriously asthmatic and, after being diagnosed and then treated with a Rife machine, he was healed of his asthma. His asthma had been related to a fungal issue and it was dealt with by vibrational frequencies. God was intentionally exposing me to things that would be a part of His direction for my life in the future. He was letting me experience things I would not understand for a long time. He was focusing my attention on the impact of emotions and the role of the physical body in our lives.

During that same time frame I was also introduced to Eye Movement Desensitization Reprocessing (EMDR), or rapid eye movement therapy.[7] I was intrigued by it because I recognized similarities between it and the brain integration therapy Brynne underwent as a toddler. She had developmental delays and repetitive speech issues that were improved, and some resolved, through a brain re-training method called Learning Links. The Learning Links method utilized crossing the midline of the body with movement and having the patient follow that movement with their eyes. EMDR, used for getting the brain "unstuck" from overwhelming trauma emotions, can be done with sound as well as vision. People respond to the stimuli of vibrations that are on the left and right side of the body, as if their eyes were moving in different directions crossing the midline of the body. Vibrations can be administered through touch or through snapping fingers. Here again, God was exposing my mind to new things to prepare me for what He had in my future. The new methods and technologies did not seem related at the time, but hindsight today tells me that God was working His plan!

During the late '90's I began asking God for keys to supernatural healing for mental disorders. David and his sister had both been diagnosed with DID (Dissociative Identity Disorder). My own life was, of course, impacted by their pain. I longed to see people with mental illnesses healed, and people with personality disorders brought into

---

[7] Francis Shapiro, PHD, *EMDR, Breakthrough Therapy* (New York: Basic Books, 1997).

wholeness and integration. After David passed I began specifically asking the Father to connect me with a healing modality that was Holy Spirit led and utilized components of EMDR. Since you have to be licensed or to have a degree to do EMDR, I knew it would be a miracle if I found something that would allow me to incorporate this tool, but I kept asking. I knew in my gut that this tool was part of the answer to bring quicker and deeper healing to people trapped by their pain.

As God brought more clients to me with sexual, physical, and emotional trauma, I knew I needed another tool that addressed both the body and the brain. So many of these folks were stuck with buried memories and were sick physically as well as emotionally. I read books like *Anatomy of the Soul*,[8] Bessel Van Der Kolk's *The Body Keeps the Score*, [9] and the aforementioned *Deadly Emotions*. These books helped confirm that there are physical patterns in the body that are connected to the after effects of trauma. These physical symptoms are often what I call, the fruit of trauma. I knew there had to be a better way to deal with the suppressed pain than talk therapy alone, or even the methods of spiritual and emotional healing known to me at that time. The people that God was sending to me were chronically traumatized and often unable to respond or engage in the types of healing prayer I was used to leading. The approaches in which I'd been trained all involved revisiting places of pain in order to receive God's healing touch and perspective. Although it worked for many, there was this group of folks for whom it was not safe. Specifically, I discovered that those with intense sexual trauma, such as victims of sex trafficking or those who had suffered intense physical abuse, were not always able to endure revisiting their trauma. Bessel Van Der Kolk, MD, head of the trauma institute in Boston, supports this understanding of trauma's impact.

---

[8] Curt Thompson, MD, *Anatomy of the Soul: Surprising connections Between Neuroscience and Spiritual Practice* (Wheaton: Tyndale Publishers, 2010).
[9] Bessel Van Der Kolk, *The Body Keeps the Score: Brain, Mind and Body in the Healing of Trauma* (USA: Penguin Books, 2014).

Then I had an experience that catapulted me into a more intensive study of the mind, body, brain, and the frequency connection. On my birthday in April of 2013, my phone started acting up. First, the sound machine on my phone quit working, ceasing to function in the middle of the night more than once. That morning, after my phone app had let me down, I sensed God saying that this was a significant occurrence, and that He was highlighting it to me. I heard the word "frequency" in my mind, and had a strong impression that the Lord wanted me to look at this word.

I went to breakfast that day with my friend Darla and shared with her what had occurred. She excitedly began sharing about her own journey, of God teaching her about frequencies. She also shared that God had given her several dreams related to frequencies. As she was talking about articles she'd researched and teachings she'd heard, I began to feel the Holy Spirit ignite my spirit with a sense of wonder and awe like I had only experienced a few times in my life. Darla gave me some video recommendations and websites to check out, and, as I left the restaurant, my clients began texting and cancelling their appointments for the day! I was able to spend the day reading articles on frequency and the body. The subject so captured my interest that for the next several months I read everything I could find on epigenetics and quantum physics. All of it was fascinating and began to give me some understanding of what I had seen and experienced. God was connecting the dots for me!

I was reminded during this season of something the Lord had whispered to me a few years back, "You are like your dad! Your interest in science is related to Me and the body I created. His focus was different, but your minds work similarly". This statement was a challenge for me to hear as I'd never thought of myself as smart like my Dad because he was a brilliant scientist and had his doctorate. But I was enthralled with the Lord's creation and fascinated with trying to understand it, just like my dad had been with chemistry and physics.

God had spoken to me through a prophet, before moving to Kansas City, that my specialty would come forth while living there. I thought my specialty was teaching and understanding severe dissociation at a deeper level, but I began to see that I was called to explore the body, soul, and spirit and how they are interrelated. Body, soul, and spirit work together! I needed this Hebraic mindset to move forward into the areas God was connecting for me.

We live in our western culture where the body, soul, and spirit are seen as separate and linear. For example, I need to lose weight, so I deal with it physically by changing my diet and exercise. However, a Hebraic mindset perceives a person's body, soul, and spirit as circular and integrated. Hebrew culture says your beliefs and emotions affect not just your body, but also your expectations and your spirit. Your unresolved emotions can affect your thoughts about losing weight or what you should eat. Everything affects everything: body, soul and spirit. Our Bible comes out of the Hebrew culture and depicts God Himself as an emotional being Who feels, a Person. His directives in Scripture indicate He sees all of life's experiences affecting all of us. Consider the following: "'God saw that it was good . . . very good" (Genesis 1:25, 31). In other words, God delighted, relished, beamed with delight over us. Or, again, consider this: "'The LORD regretted that he had made human beings on the earth, and his heart was deeply troubled" (Genesis 6:6). "[10] The Bible definitely describes God as having emotions, and He definitely directs us to love Him with ALL of ourselves.

Because we were created in his image, we too have the gift of experiencing emotions. Notice how much God talks in Proverbs about emotions affecting us: anxiety weighs the heart down; a merry heart does good like a medicine but a crushed spirit dries up the bones; a tranquil heart gives life to the flesh, but envy makes the bones rot; a joyful heart and mind are the life and health of the body.[11] Quoting from Dan Allendar's book *The Cry of the Soul*, "Listening to our

---

[10] Peter Scazzero, *Emotionally Healthy Spirituality*, Kindle Edition (Nashville: Zondervan Publishing , 2006), p 45.
[11] *Amplified Holy Bible*, Proverbs 17:22, Proverbs 18: 21.

emotions ushers us into reality and reality is where we meet God. Emotions are the language of the soul.[12]

Another quote from Dr. Joseph Mercola, a leader in natural medicine, presents clearly the effect of our emotions upon our bodies: "You cannot divorce your health from your emotions. Every feeling you have affects some part of your body, and stress can wreak havoc on your physical health—especially if you're not exercising or eating right, as both of these can help keep stress in check in the first place. Still, even if you're doing everything 'right', your emotions—both chronic and acute—can wield great power over your body."[13] Dr. Candice Pert also supports this, "Anything thinking has the whole body participating."[14] Emotions affect the whole of us, and they can affect us both positively and negatively. They can lie to us. We must depend on the Word of God!

During the 90's, God had been exposing me to different approaches to healing that I thought were strange and a bit weird. He was systematically leading me to a scientific understanding of most of these approaches. I began to grasp a fundamental truth: if it is in the body that God created, then there must be a holy purpose for it being there. He had slowly been preparing me and answering my many petitions for a tool that would go beyond just the heart and mind and include the body and the subconscious as well.

On a trip home from visiting my grandkids, a woman I had mentored contacted me, sharing excitedly that she had found a Holy Spirit led healing protocol that used components of EMDR, like I had been praying about for so long. I was a bit incredulous. She told me it was called Splankna Therapy.[15] I asked what the strange word meant. She explained it meant the deep bowels, or the subconscious, and that

---

[12] Dr. Dan Allendar and Kemper Longman, *The Cry of the Soul* (Amazon Digital Services, 2014), p 49.
[13] Joseph M. Mercola, DO, www.mercola.com
[14] Dr. Candace Pert, *Molecules of Emotion* (New York: Touchstone, 1997).
[15] Sarah Thiessen, *Splankna*, (Rockwall, TX: Crosshouse Publishing, 2011).

it was from a Greek word used multiple times in the New Testament. For example, the word Splankna, (from the verb 'splagchnizomai') is used to describe Jesus being "moved with compassion, and it can mean the gut or deep bowels."[16]

As I read about Splankna, I felt such assurance of God's leading. Here was evidence in the Bible of what God had been showing me through experience and study. The pattern God had used in the past was being repeated; God introduced me to unfamiliar areas before giving me full confirmation or understanding. It required a step of faith on my part to follow His leading, but now He was giving me confirmation in the scripture.

God had already exposed me to EFT (Emotional Freedom Technique) which involves tapping on meridian points in the body to release negative emotion. I observed a session between a dear friend and her Christian chiropractor. As I watched, my friend was healed of an incredibly traumatic incident using this tapping technique. She had tried for many years, utilizing many healing techniques to resolve her pain, but this simple tapping technique with prayer had completely released her from it. I had seen and experienced that muscle testing, or kinesiology, is incredibly accurate in defining what was good or bad for the body. Then I had been introduced to EMDR, which I'd seen bring wonderful relief of emotional pain to people. Now I was finding out that these body tools were a part of Splankna!

Splankna's methodology helps people release trauma out of the body and soul supported by the Holy Spirit and forgiveness. As I got training and began utilizing this tool, I began to see incredibly quick and significant breakthroughs in people's lives. I was able to blend my previous training in prayer work (connecting to God for His perspective on our pain) into this protocol and have been blown away at the Lord's provision for healing. His provision is so creative. There isn't one way God gives us, or one tool, for healing; there are many.

---

[16] Sarah Thiessen.

Isn't it strange how we pray and pray, and then can't believe it when what we asked for comes to fruition?

Splankna works powerfully to help people let go of old pain by helping them release subconscious and conscious emotions that are interconnected, like a root system in the garden of our heart and body. This reality is coupled with another truth, the importance of giving specific forgiveness. When we are intentional before God to release negative feelings into His hand, often the mindsets and emotions formed in the pain leave with it. It's incredible to watch and experience. For years I've watched the Holy Spirit do something similar with healing prayer models, but I also sometimes came up against people's intolerance of remembering painful experiences. Some clients were blocked by fear or dissociated body memories that they couldn't revisit or access due to their trauma's intensity. Their symptoms of fear, paralyzed emotions, or anger were an unresolved root of pain they could not re-engage. With Splankna, the suppressed or un-acknowledged memories of pain could be addressed without having to actually confront the place of pain directly. Science has indicated that our bodies have emotional memory that is stored in our cells and fascia.[17] Splankna accesses those emotion memories through prayer and muscle testing.

Our history impacts all of us whether we know it or not. Our family of origin's interactions with us set up our beliefs about God, others, and ourselves. Most researchers in psychology agree that our core beliefs about life are formed by the age of six, when we have no language but everything is felt.[18] So we all have subconsciously held belief systems that are driving some of our behaviors and responses. When we feel "triggered" into unexplained emotion, it is most often

---

[17]Paolo Tozzi, Msc, Bsc (Hons), OST, DO, PT, "Does Fascia Hold Memories?" in *Journal of Bodywork and Movement Therapies*, Vol 18, Is 2, April 2014, www.sciencedirect.com/science/article/abs/pii/S1360859213001927.
[18]Miles Nitz, MS, LMFT, "So What Exactly is A Belief System?" www.takechargecounseling.org.

some of these young, emotionally held beliefs that are the cause. We may never have had the time, resources or capacity to find out why we have reacted, but the cause often lies here in the early-formed subconscious.

Have you ever noticed that frequently, when the Lord is giving new direction or understanding about something, it seems like everywhere you go and everyone you talk to brings up the subject that God has been highlighting? For example, when you decide to get a new car, it seems that everywhere you go you see your model. Learning these new things in God, for me, was kind of like that. I would go to a coffee shop and be introduced to someone new and they would start talking about the body-soul-spirit connection, or frequency, or healing trauma. Over and over again I had these experiences, so many times that over that year I lost count! God faithfully helped me work through fearful mindsets of worry about what was New Age and what was God's design. He gave the author of Splankna, Sarah Thiessen, very clear spiritual and theological boundaries to work within so I feel complete peace using her method. The fruit of Splankna is that people experience God's life and freedom and a deeper connection to Him, coupled with the power to live differently.

I feel impressed to share here that the enemy pushes with fear and God leads with His peace. Many times through this journey I was confronted by the fear of going into deception, and each time the Lord brought new information through science or understanding through His Word and peace came.

Dealing with dissociation, my own and others, was another God-thread I didn't fully recognize for a long time (I know, you'd think I would catch on sooner!). God prepared me to deal with dissociation in my own marriage, as well as for the healing work I would one day undertake. His work of preparation began much earlier than I remembered at first. He actually introduced me to dissociation way back in high school. When I was 17 or 18 and living in New Mexico, a group of kids decided to visit Abilene Christian University to check it out during my last year of high school. There was a girl on the trip that my parents had taken under their wing. It was evident from the way she carried herself and from her withdrawn behaviors that there had been some deep wounds in her life. During the trip, I was in a room alone with her and she suddenly came at me from across the room, putting her hands on my throat. She was in a rage and I didn't know what had set her off. I was frantically praying in my mind, asking Jesus what I should do. I tried binding demons of rage and nothing changed. Suddenly I heard the Lord clearly say, "Tell her who you are." I immediately began saying, "It's me, Laurie!". After a couple of times saying it, she suddenly dropped her hands and her head, and began talking in the voice of a little girl. I was astounded and fascinated! I continued conversing with that child-like personality for a few minutes and then she returned to her normal adult self.

I had forgotten about this event until I was preparing to teach on dissociation for the Kona Counseling School with Youth With a Mission in 2013. I was asked to speak from a lay person's perspective on healing severe dissociation. Although I was functioning as a professional, seeing people full time for healing and restoration and freedom, it didn't change the fact that I wasn't licensed as a counselor. Even so, I was being asked to impart insight in this arena. Only God! I was asked to return the following year to speak on the body-soul-spirit inter-connection. My friend Ashley, who also had been on a journey to understand the way God designed us and how emotions affect us, partnered with me this time. Until this season, though I read Proverbs multiple times a year, I never realized how often the scriptures talked about the power of our emotions and thoughts. I was coming into a fresh understanding of this truth from all God was teaching me.

As I began looking back at my history of God introducing me to those with severe trauma and fractured identities, it was astounding how consistently He brought these hurting people into my life. My husband David and his sister Nitzy were two, but there were countless others as well. I would be their friend or I would be part of a prayer group that was supporting their healing journey, when we would encounter patterns of behaviors that prohibited them from breaking free. Time and time again it became clear that they had splintered into other personalities. For His own purposes, the Father had given me an ability to make people suffering from inner pain feel safe. For a number of years in my 20's I actually wondered if these people were seeking me out because I'd been fractured or split myself. I didn't understand why these people kept being drawn to me! Finally I was able to see that my own dissociation from my dad's death, a condition that existed in my soul for over twenty years, was the piece that gave me an understanding of those struggling further down the scale of dissociation. Because my mom remarried and moved us five months after my dad died, I had put a lid on my pain and memories, locking them deep inside. I didn't deal with this dissociation of my grief until I was in my 30's!

God in His kindness arranged circumstances so that David and I were provided with some counseling after one of his infidelities. We were asked at a counseling center to take the Taylor Johnson assessment, which is a long profile. In the session that followed the assessment, to my chagrin, the counselor let me know that I was not very in touch with myself. He said something to the effect of, "Laurie, you have unfortunately invalidated your assessment due to your very strong denial mechanisms". This confrontive but kind statement made me feel as though I'd been hit by a truck, but it was the catalyst for me to begin getting in touch with my locked up pain from years before. It was the beginning of my awareness of my own denial connected to the first 31 years of my life. It was when I began to let myself grieve my father's death, and many other losses and betrayals. We all can dissociate at the most basic levels, compartmentalizing things we don't feel equipped to deal with. We tuck the pain away inside where we believe it's not affecting us, but the truth is that it is still impacting all of us, both consciously and unconsciously. The problem is the pain "leaks" out eventually in one form or another. Denial, or the unwillingness to acknowledge that you have a problem, cannot only hurt you for the long run but it can also wall you off from others by blocking your ability to connect with people. The plain truth is that you can't be healed of stuff you aren't willing to look at.

Each time I was in relationship with someone who was "split" or severely dissociated, I learned something new. Each exposure to others coping with trauma this way, was helpful in preparing me to cope with David's struggle. Understanding that God was teaching me, gave me perspective and grace to walk with David through his journey of healing from sexual abuse, and the subsequent integration of his fractured soul parts. We had outside counselors to support and guide us, but living with a person with DID is a hard, up-and-down emotional journey. Again, it took years for me to realize that my experiences as a teen and then my own dysfunction, were all part of God's plan to later use me to help other people cope with trauma and come into healing. I have come to believe emphatically that there are no coincidences when you follow Jesus!

During the many years when God repeatedly shut the door on my getting a degree, He would tell me, "I'm going to teach you through non-traditional means". I didn't understand God's training methods and their advantages and limitations for many years. But these past few years when so many licensed counselors are restricted in presenting Biblical perspectives for healing of one's sexual identity (which I deal with frequently), I am not, because I'm not under the mandates of licensure. I also believe that had I gone the more traditional route, God would not have received as much glory as I have been able to give to Him with having no degree. I minister under His favor for His purposes.

Don't misunderstand me, please. I love people going into Psychology and other professional avenues of therapy! We need these professions, and I refer to those with licensure, but it was not my calling to go that route. We serve an awesome Creator and Redeemer and He truly has given us all we need for life and godliness. He is always leading us with His eye on us to accomplish His unique purpose through us and in us, even when we don't recognize it. His ways and His thoughts are higher than ours.[19]

For a number of years I received a strong impression repeatedly from the Lord that I was to live a fasted lifestyle. I kept asking Him what He meant but received no more clarity for several years. I asked Him if He meant doing without certain foods, or doing without certain amenities, but nothing seemed to land. So I kept making excuses for the way I functioned, over working and then indulging in whatever I felt like eating. Later, as I came to understand the impact of cumulative trauma on the body and the impact of ongoing stress on the body, I realized that the Father was trying to protect me, not restrict me. He was saying, "Live a fasted life" because He knew that all of the trauma I had throughout my life was going to have a negative cumulative effect on my body. He knew I needed to eat healthier and get more rest in order for my body to maintain health. He wasn't a killjoy!

Symptoms of inflammation and random pain throughout my body began in 2009. By the time I moved to Kansas City, I was attempting to make the appropriate changes in my diet to support more overall strength and health, but I'd waited too long and the symptoms just kept coming.

Science is now seeing a correlation between autoimmune disorders and trauma that is unresolved long term.[20] Starting in the 2000's, I worked to diligently examine the root issues in my heart and to resolve buried pain, but my body was yelling loudly at me for not dealing with these issues sooner. Changing my diet to non-inflammatory foods has helped, but because I waited until the symptoms were constant, I am paying the price of not heeding the Father's warning sooner. He is meeting me with help and insight through doctors and friends, but I

---

[19] *Amplified Holy Bible*, Isaiah 55:9-10, "As far as the heavens are higher than the earth, so are my thoughts higher than your thoughts."
[20] "Can Trauma Trigger Rheumatoid Arthritis and Other Autoimmune Diseases?", www.EverydayHealth.com (June, 2018).

really do think if I had listened and come under His constraints sooner, I may not have experienced these issues to the degree I am physically.

Where in your journey has the Father's directive been and you possibly haven't recognized it? Where are there threads of continuity that you haven't realized were His tying things together? He isn't just doing this for me! He's always bringing truth and revelation to us if we invite it. I've been on a learning curve for years that was preparing me for what I was to do in this season, and to do it with excellence, confidence, and partnership with the Holy Spirit. What is the Father wanting to show you or help you understand that you may not have seen or comprehended? He's not limited by our time and He's always leading us and revealing things for His purpose.

Father God, would you make me aware of all the ways You have taught me and protected me and led me into Your purposes? I want to thank You for Your gracious heart toward me and Your patience with the things I don't see or understand. Make me aware of Your leading through the patterns of continuity in my life and through Your Word. Bring understanding and revelation to me of the things You have created me for, that only I can do or be! Help me connect the dots you are presenting. Lead me with Your eye on me.

The week that I had all the revelation about frequency, this song came to me in the car, of all places! I am continually filled with joy and awe at the wonder of the creation of our brains and bodies!

Nothing about You is random
All You do has intention
The sun, moon and stars and the rhythm of earth
How we're created, our cells and our birth - a detailed design

Creation is in divine order
Your Word holds all things together

Genius displayed in the sounds of the earth
Vibrations of beauty declaring Your worth --- a Masterpiece!

We are awestruck, Holy One
Awestruck by Your power, none compares beside You,
God, You reign
We are awestruck, Holy One
Awestruck by Your strength, none compares beside You
God, You reign

You are Creator, our Redeemer
There is none like You
You are a wonder
There's no other
Lord of all the earth
You are a wonder
There's no other
Lord of the universe
Laurie Goddu ©

Chapter 3: Expectation is Invitation

Often we don't understand how consistently the enemy has set us up for fear, and that fear is his significant tool for undermining our faith and obedience. I recently was sharing with a therapist here in Kansas City that I used to think shame was at the core of every dysfunction, but that my recent conclusion was that Satan's most common tool is fear. At the very least, shame and fear are always working together. They are both powerful emotions that keep us from moving forward into all God has for us. I have walked in a deep measure of healing from shame in my identity, but I still have to address fear regularly. These tools or spirits from Satan came in with sin in the Garden of Eden and have been hindering mankind ever since.

The fear of not being enough, the fear of failure, the fear that God won't come through, the fear of not being heard, the fear of being invalidated or victimized --- there are thousands of fears. If the enemy gets us to partner with fear, he doesn't have to hang around. We become frozen or constricted when we entertain fearful thoughts, and fear can affect how we approach life and relationships. It causes us to hold onto control instead of letting God be in control. Shame keeps us from living from our true identity in Christ, but fear can be just as paralyzing as shame, and it is contrary to faith.

Science has discovered that we are an influence in our own life-journeys for success or failure. We are neither pawns nor victims. The truth of our influence over our own destiny is rooted in Biblical truth. The writer of Proverbs tells us that "death and life are in the power of the tongue, and those who love it will eat its fruit and bear the consequences of their words."[21] This passage emphasizes that what we say is important because our words reflect what we believe. Jesus Himself said that a person speaks "out of that which fills his heart."[22]

Much has been written on the power of positive thinking. The New Age Movement has taken this idea to mean that we are demi-gods who decide our own destinies. This kind of mind-over-matter thinking is not Christianity. The Creator of all life is intricately involved in our lives and destinies but He also gave us a brain, a tongue, and the ability to choose what we believe. We have the power to partner with God Himself for great things! He says that He is able to do abundantly more than we dare to ask or think, infinitely beyond our greatest prayers, hopes and dreams.[23] He gave us the power in our hearts and in our mouths to bring about righteous change, to impact the world with our faith and with our words.

There are countless numbers of people who are living examples of the transformation that faith can work in a life, people who have hoped and believed for the impossible. Science also supports the constructive effect of positive words. Research has discovered that positive words such as peace and love alter our genes' expression while negative words activate the amygdala (fear center of the brain).[24]

---

[21] *Amplified Holy Bible*, Proverbs 18:21.

[22] *New King James Bible*, Luke 6:45 (Nashville: Thomas Nelson Publishing Company, 1982).

[23] *Amplified Holy Bible*, Ephesians 3:20

[24] Andrew Newberg, MD and Mark R. Waldman, *Words Can Change Your Brain* (London: Penguin Books, 2012).

The opposite of faith is fear, and fear was a constant in my life from an early age. Fear combatted my faith with regularity. Since my dad died suddenly, with no warning, when I was twelve, I lived in the fear of something bad happening to me or to my family. The fear of being a disappointment was almost as big since I came out of a very performance-oriented background.

My late husband's pattern of infidelity, and his ensuing death from lung cancer, fueled these fears. More traumas and betrayals of various kinds in my close circle added to my fears. I wanted to believe God is Who He says He is, but my heart and mind lived in doubt, not faith. I, like many Christians, stated with my mouth that I trusted Him, but my heart was not in alignment at the core of my being. I lived in a state I call "the grey zone," meaning that what I allowed myself to feel was kept in a "safe zone," a place where I didn't expect too much, so that if nothing good happened I wouldn't have far to fall. Somehow I felt this was a better way to live. I rationalized that if I didn't expect anything, the disappointment wouldn't be as severe. The Bible says that we can't please God without faith and we can't overcome without faith. Without realizing it, what I was operating in was unbelief.

The Father was so kind to challenge me on this mindset and to expose how much I lived there. Over and over again He invited me to live in the expectation that He wanted good for me and that He wanted to answer my heart's desires. This process was many years long, and involved looking at many different areas where fear was affecting me --- fear of disappointing others, fear that I'd be rejected because I wasn't good enough, fear that God would hold out on me because I'd failed, fear that I was too much. I'm finally living in a place where these beliefs are faint in my head, but freedom has come only after I rejected the old mindsets and received God's truth about Who He says I am, and Who He says He is: God is for us and He loves us unconditionally. Acquiring this freedom has also been a process of moving from wanting to believe things into truly knowing this is what God wants for me. This knowing is assurance and this is faith.

One huge fear I addressed was fear that I would never get married again. It included the fear that I'd disappoint God if I wanted to remarry. I wanted to please Him but I feared that I wouldn't be loving Him as well if I had a husband. I worked through many skewed beliefs about marriage before I aligned my heart and mind with the knowledge that God is for us as His daughters and sons. He desires to meet our longings and needs. His original design is for partnership in marriage. The Lord had me meditate in Psalm 37 for almost a year, to build my faith in the many truths in this passage. Over and over I meditated on this powerful chapter:" Dwell in the land and do good. Delight yourself in the Lord and He will give you the desires and petitions of your heart."[25]

I have encountered many clients that were hope-deferred in their waiting for a mate and they literally felt frozen or numb in their unbelief. As we worked through lies they believed about themselves and removed barriers they had towards the Lord, many of them were engaged or married within a year of the sessions. Letting go of agreement with beliefs such as "no one will love me for me", or "Men aren't trustworthy," "I'm not good enough for a man," "God answers others' prayers but not mine", has the potential to open up your future to God's provision and breakthrough. Letting go of lies releases faith and an expectation of God's answering.

Another fear surfaced concerning money after David passed. The life insurance money that was mine upon his death brought significant provision, but the funds were dwindling quickly and this brought anxiety. Even with no huge splurges, just college funds, raising four kids, and doing life was draining the bank account quickly. I began struggling with shame, shame that I had not managed the money well, shame over not being a good steward of God's resources, and the fear of being judged as a failure. I heard the word "failure" over and over on the inside. I was convinced others would judge me and deem me unfit as a good steward.

---

[25] *Amplified Holy Bible*, Psalm 37:3-5.

Even with giving much to the Kingdom with joy, ongoing struggles with being unable to sell my home, plus my inability to keep to a budget, kept my fears entrenched. Then 2008 happened and, like many, I lost a large chunk in the market crash. Loss happened to millions of others, not just me, and it wasn't because of anything that we had done, but this was a turning point for me in dealing with my fear.

I remember one morning standing on my back porch praying about the future and my dwindling funds, and the Holy Spirit whispered, "Will you still trust me when the monies are gone?" Surprised by the question, I initially replied, "No," then lamented "I don't know how Lord. Will You work in me to trust You here?" He was faithful to answer that cry. It meant voicing my shame and fear to others. Every time I shared what I was battling, others' gracious responses helped change my view of myself. God didn't see me as a failure!

Over the next few years, I faced the choice numerous times, to reject the voice of shame and fear and trust the Father's provision. I also learned to look for God's wisdom to manage what He was giving me now. The insurance money ended up lasting 10 years, until 2012. By that time, I actually found that I had more faith to believe Him for daily provision than I did when I had money in the account!

Don't allow the enemy to paralyze you with fear of what might happen! There is no grace for living a life focused on the future, only grace for the present. Rest in the knowledge that He is with us in trouble and He is our help. While there were continuing financial challenges due to a variety of accidents and illnesses, particularly with my daughter, there were many supernatural places of provision for Brynne and me so that my faith grew by leaps and bounds.

One day in 2012 I had run out of funds in the bank and needed $1000 to pay the rent and bills. I was driving up north of the city to see a client from out of town. Instead of Skyping with me to do ministry, she had chosen to fly to town to do the work. I was still only receiving an offering for my time with clients. Sometimes those offerings were on the low end; at other times they were significant gifts. On the drive to see this client, I prayed out loud, "Father, You are my Husband and Provider. You know I need $1000 in the next three days! Please help!"

Upon meeting my new client, she turned to me and announced she was paying me for her time. I let her know I wasn't expecting payment until the conclusion of our time, but she responded emphatically that she wanted to pay me first. She then proceeded to pull out $1000 in cash from her purse. I was astonished! I became teary and shared my earlier prayer, thanking her profusely for the gift. It was more than I had ever been given by anyone for a week's worth of ministry. Although it felt disproportionate to what I gave to her, she was the Father's provision for me, so I received it with joy and humility. I couldn't remember ever before experiencing this kind of extravagant, immediate provision in answer to a prayer for a financial need. Wow! The God of the Universe was truly listening and aware of my every need.

While ministering to another single mom, another supernatural provision occurred. The Holy Spirit impressed me to give her my savings. It was only $250.00, but it was all I had. After arguing with Him for several minutes that, "this wasn't wise", He gently kept nudging me. Then He reminded me of the story of the widow being provided with oil by Elisha told in 2 Kings 4. I could not ignore that He was saying, so I told the woman what the Lord had said. She rejected my offer saying she couldn't possibly take my money. I asked her to ask God whether she was to receive it. When she asked, she heard God say, "Yes." The look on her face was priceless! A week later I received an unexpected gift of $500, double the amount I had given her! God opened His hand to satisfy our need.

The Bible says, "Cast your bread upon the water, for you will find it after many days.[26]In that season of growing a business and depending on God for referrals, I grew in such peace about finances as God provided for every need in creative ways. I would not have grown into faith and an expectation of His provision if I had not been challenged

---

[26] *Amplified Holy Bible*, Ecclesiastes 11:1.

to do so. Just like we have to engage our muscles physically to build strength, we have to use our faith muscles for them to become strong.

My most chronic fear has been the fear of man and the fear of disappointing others. As long as I can remember I have fought the feeling that I was never enough, or the opposite feeling, that I was too much. God presented me with many opportunities to crush this fear under my feet. I didn't always succeed, but when I did, it was by pushing through the fear and embracing truth, which means responding differently. For instance, when I would read others' faces and wonder if they were upset with me, instead of allowing the swirl of anxiety to take hold, I'd approach them and ask if they had any need that I could pray with them for. I turned my focus away from me and the insecurity I felt, and towards serving and helping others. I determined that I would "kick the enemy's teeth in" concerning the spirit of fear, according to Psalm 3 where it says that "the enemy's teeth will be shattered", (this is the Laurie translation).

Fear can manifest in a myriad of ways. When I was younger and struggled with not feeling valid, I exaggerated statements, hoping that the magnification would somehow bring value to me and prove I was good enough. I was also set up by my family as this was a normal in their everyday language. Exaggerating became such a habit that I was unaware of it except for the lingering fear that I would get caught. Finally the exposure I'd feared happened, but it was for my good!

I had invited those in my close circle to call me out if they thought I might be exaggerating. One day while traveling with David we stopped at a hotel. As I entered the bathroom, I yelled, "Oh no, there are three huge roaches in the bathtub!" David quietly asked from the other room, "How many roaches are there, Laurie?" I responded sheepishly, "Two big roaches." Then David quietly asked again, "How many roaches are there? And how big are they?" This time I croaked out my answer in true humiliation, "There is one and it's only this big," while indicating towards the tip of my finger. Was this humbling? Yes! But this was the beginning of the end for me changing. It was hard and it was scary, but in addressing my pattern head-on, over time I became free of the fear of being exposed. Now I chuckle at this memory.

God uses even the hard stuff to prepare and mold and teach us; this is the way He works. He used an event one Easter morning to bring me to a deeper trust in His protection of me. I'd had a chronic fear as a child of being assaulted, but had overcome it as an adult. I walked alone daily, without being nervous. I'd pray and worship and even sing out loud sometimes as I walked. This particular Easter morning was different from my normal outing as the neighborhood was devoid of people walking or mowing their yards. It was very unusual for me to be so alone as I walked, as many neighbors usually were out in the early morning hours.

I was more than halfway through my walk, when a man on a motorcycle slowly entered my horseshoe-shaped neighborhood. I could see his blond curls below his helmet and noted his red t-shirt. I did the head nod and kept on going, singing in the Spirit. As I started up the next street, I was startled by the voice of the Holy Spirit sternly and loudly saying, "Put your head down!" I'd never had Him "yell" at me before! I immediately obeyed, even though I didn't understand. Within seconds I could hear a motorcycle moving towards me, just around the bend. I was now on alert, as I knew the neighborhood well, and it was literally impossible that he could have cut across the horseshoe without speeding up a lot. The same man on the motorcycle very slowly passed me, with the sound of his bike idling low and near. I kept my head down and increased my pace.

As I approached a slight curve in the road, I burst into a sprint. I cut across a yard in front of me and to the left and visually eyed where I could hide. I was not going to look over my shoulder to see if he was following. I saw a very large bush in front of the porch of the house next door. I ducked down quickly, with my breathing heavy and fast. Then I heard the sound of the motorcycle coming back my direction.

I jumped into action and pounded on the door of the house. It felt like forever before a woman's face peered through the curtain on the door. I said urgently, "There's a man on a motorcycle following me and he's coming! Would you please let me in or call the police?" She could see the fear on my face, and hear the intensity in my voice as she opened the door a few inches.

"Do you hear that?" I asked. She acknowledged the sound of the bike and began dialing 911. She then let me slip in the front door. We waited together as we first heard, then saw the motorcyclist slowly come up her street looking for me. I was shaking like a leaf, but slowly the guy turned around and left.

Within minutes the police arrived. After taking my statement, they acknowledged that they had passed the guy leaving the area as they came in. One of the officers affirmed I'd done the right thing. He stated there was a rapist in the area fitting this guy's description who had been using a knife on his victims, and he had not been caught yet.

Later that day, I realized that what I'd just experienced, God had warned me about several months before. I'd had a very vivid dream that had three scenes. I won't go into all the details, but in the conclusion of the dream there had been a warning. In the final scene I was alone and the enemy exposed himself to me by pulling out a knife and saying he was going to kill me. I woke up with that image in my mind. I presented the dream to several others skilled in interpreting dreams. They all agreed that the Holy Spirit was telling me not to discount His voice, particularly in public, and to obey it immediately. They also felt an assault from the enemy was coming in the future. I never imagined that the dream might be literal, but it had been, and God had me prepared.

After this event my son-in-law bought me a gun and my son Collin helped me learn to shoot. I carried that gun with me for a couple of years as that experience made me uneasy about walking alone. Eventually I was able to be comfortable leaving the gun at home when I walked. The fear of being assaulted was conquered as I applied the verse from Psalm 56:3, "When I am afraid I will trust in You," along with other scriptures I memorized. There's nothing wrong with having physical protection, but your final trust has to be in the Lord. Listen to God and don't discount the things He shows you, even when you don't understand. If God gives you a warning, it is to prepare you, not push you with fear. His warning brings an alertness and establishes your trust that He is going before you.

God continued to kindly address fears and lowered expectations in multiple areas of my life. He was on a mission to help set me free so the enemy didn't have a foothold in my life. When we found out we were living with mold in our basement apartment, God provided a place through another single woman for Brynne and me to live and from which I could work while remediation went on. During that month-long stay in her home, I had a significant encounter with the Father that would bring a revelation to me that radically strengthened my faith.

I had done a live interview at my local church a few weeks before and they had given me a gift card to a famous barbecue place as a thank you for my sharing. I went to pick up my order one evening and, upon arriving home, found that the meat portion of the order was wrong. I immediately called the restaurant and was told to return and they would fix the order. I was greeted at the take-out counter by a young man who gave me the new order.

As I confirmed that the meat portions had been corrected, he gruffly stated that the entire order had been replaced. I was so surprised, and turned to leave, feeling a bit dazed. Then a manager approached, calling me by name. "Miss Morris? I want to apologize for the mix up you had with your order, and to ensure that you will visit us again. I'd like to give you a $50 gift certificate." I was dumbfounded! As I walked away from the restaurant, I felt almost giddy with wonder. "What the heck?" I began muttering under my breath to the Lord, "That's crazy! That's way too much to give me in exchange. Double the order? That's ridiculous!"

As clear as day the Father immediately said, "That's the way I love you --- ridiculously over the top, I want to give you good gifts and satisfy you!" I began to laugh and cry at the same time, as this revelation of His Father-heart for me began to invade my entire being. I was overcome with the knowledge of His desire to give me what I needed with joy. That day was a turning point for me. My confidence shifted from an "I'm less than", fear-based approach, to having complete assurance that God joyfully wanted to answer my heart's desires.

What's so crazy is that at least a year before this, the Lord had said something to me in a time of listening prayer. I heard the old Carly Simon song, "Anticipation," in my head.[27] At the time, I'd written in my journal: "Anticipation is making me wait, but it feels really good. I feel my excitement growing like a little kid's. It's gonna be so good." Jesus had impressed on me that day, "This is a key word for you Laurie." He showed me that I'd been anticipating the next disappointment instead of His provision. His direction was, "I want you to anticipate the man I have for you with delight that I'm bringing you a man of stature. You've been approaching it the wrong way. Anticipate Me like a child waiting for Daddy to give you a treat. I always keep My word."

God's words had been an encouragement to me, similar to when He said, "I love you ridiculously" but I had completely forgotten the "anticipation" word and it hadn't taken root in my soul. God is so kind to reiterate His truth to us. Sometimes we need to hear it over and over until we get it, but that is not frustrating to Him. Just think of how often this happened with the Israelites! He faithfully and consistently challenged me on changing my lowered expectations. He asked me to let go of the fear of being disappointed and when I finally let go, I was propelled into real faith and confidence, faith that He is working for my good. I had numerous opportunities to choose to come into agreement with His words to me, that He is for me, that He has good things for me. I began to see a new normal created in my thinking and in my experience through the change in my expectations.

The world of science and epigenetics is proving more and more that the way God made the body intricately wonderful and full of capacity to work for itself. As I said earlier, our minds, and our words, are much

---

[27] Carly Simon, "Anticipation" performed and written by Carly Simon for Elektra Records, 1971.

more powerful than we realize. Dr. Caroline Leaf teaches on the power of our agreements and the value of aligning our emotions with the scriptures. She states, "Research shows that as much as 87% of illnesses can be attributed to our thought life. Studies conclusively link more chronic diseases to an epidemic of toxic emotions in our culture."[28] She teaches in several of her books that we can change the way we think; we can align our thoughts with God's truth. These choices can be a catalyst for change in several areas of our lives, even our health and our circumstances. It takes time and repetition but the brain does change and our heart can change with it.[29]

Scientists have discovered that our thoughts, emotions and expectations can even influence our DNA. Human beliefs and perceptions toward the environment, both positive and negative, impact our genes.[30] The study of the mind, its influence in the development of the brain, as well as its influence upon our relationships, now has a name --- interpersonal neurobiology.[31] I'm highlighting this so that we understand that what we feel and say and believe with strong intention, has influence in the outcome of our lives and relationships over time.

We should not be surprised when the scripture talks about hope and expectations a lot. Hope is mentioned 129 times in the Bible. Expect is mentioned over 40 times. The Father wants us to agree with His heart, and His heart is full of positive things for us He wants us to believe that He desires to bring us breakthroughs and to fulfill His promises. He wants us to live honestly before Him and to ask for His help where we are weak, expecting Him to answer.

---

[28] Dr. Caroline Leaf, *Who Switched Off My Brain?* (USA: Switch On Your Brain USA, 2008) p. 5.

[29] Dr. Caroline Leaf, *Who Switched Off My Brain?*

[30] Bruce Lipton, PhD, *The Biology of Belief* (USA, Hay House Publishing, 2008).

[31] Curt Thompson MD, *Anatomy of the Soul*, Kindle Edition (Wheaton: Tyndale Publishing, 2010), p.362.

Father, I repent of living in that grey space of not really expecting anything. I've been stuck in my fear of nothing changing. I'm sick of living like this. I want to thrive and be filled with anticipation for the future. I want to believe that Your heart is for me and Your hand is open to me. Give me what I need, Holy Spirit. Enable me to believe and ask in faith for what my heart longs. I reject the lies that I've partnered with. I give you the negative emotions I have felt. I choose to trust in Who You Are and not just what I've experienced or felt. According to Romans 12:1, I choose to renew my mind daily and submit my body to You and ask for Your transformation in me, to bring me into agreement with Your will. Help me water Your truth in my mind so that it takes root. Help me believe Ephesians 3:20 that you will answer super abundantly! How do You want to align me with truth and heal my heart and mind, Father?

Your mercy brings healing, Your truth is a sword
Cutting asunder the lies of our souls
Truth shall spring up, from the earth below
Righteousness looks down from heaven

They meet and kiss, Truth and love
Your revelation flows
They meet and kiss, the Spirit's touch
The Truth transforming us

Your living Word, changing our hearts
Now we can hear clearly
Your living Word, changing our hearts
Now we see what You see

They meet and kiss, Truth and love
Your revelation flows
They meet and kiss, the Spirit's touch

The Truth transforming us

Now we see what You see
You see us whole
Laurie Goddu ©

Chapter 4: Perspectives on Unanswered Prayer: Is God good?

God is always working for our good! It's a paradox of the Kingdom that God is a redeemer of all things. He takes the painful life situations in our lives and works in such a way that they somehow end up producing something beautiful. How in the world does this happen? I don't know. It's a mystery. But if we resolve our hearts to believe in His redemption of all things, He will show Himself true. James 1:2-5 says, "Consider it nothing but joy, my brothers and sisters, whenever you fall into various trials. Be assured that the testing of your faith [through experience] produces endurance [leading to spiritual maturity, and inner peace]. And let endurance have its perfect result, so that you may be perfect and completely developed [in your faith], lacking in nothing."[32] When we are hurting and experiencing hard things, we all tend to forget this verse.

I've seen so many miracles in my journey. But I've also experienced what appears to be unanswered prayer and there is often suffering attached to it. The question is: are those prayers really, truly

---

[32] *Amplified Holy Bible,* James 1:2-5.

unanswered? Or are we seeing from too narrow a perspective? Do we assume we know the best way for the prayer to be answered? Are we sometimes disappointed when God doesn't do things our way, or in "our time frame", forgetting that God is not limited as we are and has methods which are impossible for us to conceive? His ways are not our ways.

For many years I have fought to overcome the feeling that I was a particularly hard case for God. I felt that God had to use painful things to teach me a lesson because I was such a mess. This imprint was even more strongly ingrained by the circumstances of loss and difficulties I experienced in my journey. I came to believe in my painful experiences (and my evaluation of them) more than in what the Father said in the Bible and in His voice to me personally. He said that His heart was for me and that His purposes for me were good, but I was hurting. Over and over again, He gently wooed me with the truth in His Word, to resolve in my mind and heart that He was always working for my good.

The revelation that God was not necessarily wanting the hard things for me brought about a huge shift in my belief system. Outwardly, and even with my words, I had proclaimed Romans 8:28 to be my life verse, that "God [who is deeply concerned about us] causes all things to work together [as a plan] for good for those who love God, to those who are called according to His plan and purpose."[33] But the fruit of disappointments in life led me to feel disappointed with God and to mistrust Him. Questions of "why, and how could You?" persisted. This cycle was indicative that there was not a settled belief in His goodness in my heart. Where there is a symptom, there is a cause or where there is a fruit, there is a root. My doubt and unbelief was not good fruit!

Resolution for my questioning heart came rather recently through my experiencing a dear friend's agonizing loss. My friends had waited on God for years, believing to conceive a child. During the week of my birthday that year, I found out with the rest of their friends and family, that the baby they'd prayed for and eagerly anticipated was stillborn.

---

[33] *Amplified Holy Bible*, Romans 8:28.

There had been no indication that something was wrong in her pregnancy. I was outraged at God. I knew they had partnered in prayer over that child daily like very few people I'd known. "What the heck did You just let happen God?" was my thought that day. I'd taken off work to celebrate my birthday and felt the Lord impress on me to go see the movie, Do You Believe.[34] I was not excited. I haven't particularly enjoyed Christian flicks in the past, and I was still in shock over my friend's loss. I grudgingly asked my housemate Ashley if she'd go with me.

As we entered and chose our seats, we realized we were the only two people in the theater. From the get-go I felt the Lord talking to me through the story. I began quietly crying, then eventually sobbing, as the story unfolded and I knew that Heaven was challenging me. Thank goodness the Lord was kind enough to allow us to be the only two people in the theater since I was such a blubbering mess!

Without going into the plot, the ending was clearly about perspectives, our earthly frame of reference versus God's eternal one. God is wholly other and not limited by our time or space, while we are earthly beings, living each moment in a specific time and place. I repented deeply for the judgments I had made toward the Father with my accusations through the years. This was far from the first time, I had repented for this, but this time felt different; God had gotten to my core. I committed to the Lord that I would no longer question His hand and His ways. I resolved in my heart that He is always working for my good, in trouble, in pain and loss, even when I don't understand or when it appears that He has not answered. I resolved to wait and trust and watch Him weave a tapestry of redemption in my life. As I repented, a fresh revelation came, then certainty, that God cannot be unfaithful! He is all goodness and light, and faithful is Who He Is.

Later that week, after attending the funeral of my friend's little one, another friend and I visited with the mother, Rebecca, and her

---

[34] Jon Gunn, director, "Do You Believe?" Motion Picture (USA:Pure Flix Studio, March 2015 release).

husband. I asked them how they were doing so well in the midst of such tragedy. They were in profound agony, but trusting God fully. She vulnerably shared a dream she'd had years before that was bringing comfort and clarity in their tragedy. As she told me and my friend her dream, I felt the presence of the Holy Spirit and the Father's weeping heart towards hard things, "What is about to happen I do not want but it must be," was the clear impression I had in that moment.

I was deeply impacted by Rebecca's dream and by my interactions with her. The experience reconfirmed the commitment I had made to the Father a few days before, and it settled me in a way that has never shifted in the years since. God is good and His ways are perfect.

In the ensuing years, another woman of God's take on the goodness of God came into my world through the voice of Joni Erickson Tada. Joni, a quadriplegic for over 50 years, says, "God hates what He allows in order to accomplish that which He loves." [35] She lives in the place of faith described by these words and displays more confident trust and joy than anyone I've ever met, despite constant pain and hardship physically. God can and will give us what we need to trust Him, even when it feels impossible.

The trustworthiness of God is emphasized in the Bible's account of Abraham and his son, Isaac, found in Genesis 22:1-14. God commanded Abraham to sacrifice his only son, Isaac. Abraham obeyed, built an altar, and placed Isaac on it; but God displayed Himself as the God Who Provides and gave Abraham a ram to sacrifice instead. "What God requires He will provide," is the meaning of God's name in the passage, Jehovah Jireh. "In the mountain of the Lord, what God requires, He will provide," verse 14.

In Joni's case and millions of others around the world, in our moment of greatest trial or need, God has shown up with provision. Whether it was physical provision like the ram, or equipping with strength or emotional resilience, or giving insight or revelation, or

---

[35] Joni Erikkson-Tada of Joni and Friends Ministry, Agoura Hills, CA.

expanding our capacity, whatever our lack, God provides for us to fulfill His purposes in our lives

Perhaps the hardest circumstance of seemingly unanswered prayer for me was my late husband's death. My personality and inclination is to want to understand the why's of life, to try to find a reason for the hardship. However, sometimes full understanding is simply not achievable. We both separately heard the Lord say to us that David would be healed here on earth. Obviously this didn't happen as he is in heaven. I don't think I'll ever know the full answer to this. Was it our mis-hearing? Or lack of faith? I don't know even today what the correct answer is. What I do know, and settle my heart with, is that we didn't do something wrong. We were in trouble and cried out to God for help. He did bring that, just not in the way we were expecting.

As I shared in my book, *Shattered, and Then...*, I do believe that David's agreement with shame was an open door for the enemy to use for harm at some level. He could not or would not let the Lord's provision of grace cover and wash away his shame connected to his sexual struggles and history. Thus, though there were thousands praying and fasting for his healing, he remained in agreement with the accusation that there was something wrong with him because of his moral failures. He held onto his sin, believing it was bigger than God's mercy. As stated before, our personal beliefs deeply impact our lives for negative or positive outcomes. God's Word supports that there is power in our agreement, for life or for death. Faith can move mountains, and faith in the negative, or faith in the lie, can constrain us, block us, and cause damage.

Right after David passed, there was a group of committed, praying friends and elders, who asked if they could pray and fast to raise him from the dead. I was fine with them doing that, but I had no faith to believe for it. I gave permission and they committed themselves to intense prayer and fasting before the night of his viewing. Nothing happened that we could tell, but we don't know if David was given a chance to say yes to those prayers calling him back. We have no idea what went on after his spirit left His body to meet Jesus. Often stories

57

of those who have passed and come back to life, state that they were given the choice of staying with Jesus or returning to earth. None of us will ever know the battle my late husband faced every day to maintain his freedom from his past sexual imprints. He just might have said no to the offer to return to earth. We simply don't know, so to say that there wasn't enough faith is not a healthy response.

For almost seven years I was choosing to obey the Holy Spirit's direction to pray for others who were ill even though I really was not in alignment with faith for physical healing. In those years, I didn't see miracles with my eyes, but my faith muscles were activated by my obedience. Eventually I did see a miracle --- a man many of us had been crying out for was healed. Since that time, I've seen incredible miracles of healing regularly in the emotional realm, and many physical healings as well. I've known people with cancer that were healed without medicine and with medicine. I've worked with people who were healed of bi-polar disorder and no longer need meds. I have seen people who couldn't get pregnant, get pregnant. I've had clients healed of severe back pain as they simultaneously released their emotional pain. I had one client healed of pain during intimacy after an agonizing several years of pain. I and another friend did work with her that unlocked very old birth trauma. The delay and the process of healing unlocked the body. Don't despair in waiting for God's process to produce a good work. Keep asking and keep believing! Sometimes delays to answers are divinely purposeful for healing in other areas of our lives.

Looking back on my childhood, when I had to move at crucial ages, I experienced what seemed like unanswered prayer. Eventually I saw the Father's redemption in those difficult moves. The first time was when my mom remarried after my dad's death and we moved from Michigan, where I was born, to Indiana. Everything I knew and loved was being left in Michigan and I felt completely helpless and lost. I couldn't fathom how God could work something good out of such sadness and loss.

God did not answer my prayers to stop the move or the remarriage; however, within months of arriving in Indianapolis, I was invited to go on a bike outreach with a Methodist youth group. On a break in our ride, a youth leader shared the truth of the gospel and the personal invitation Jesus has for us to be born again. It was the first time anyone had told me in a way I could understand that Jesus was waiting for me to ask Him to be Lord. I acknowledged my need of Him as a Savior. I was radically transformed on that day, and knew without a shadow of a doubt that Jesus now lived in me! I don't know when or where or how this would have happened in my life living in Michigan. My vulnerability from loss opened my heart to my desperate need of a Savior. Only God! He made something beautiful out of that hard season for me.

During that time, my stepsister Julie and my grandma also came to know Jesus through my testimony of His reality. Grandma has been gone for a long time and Julie has also recently gone to be with Jesus. I'm forever grateful for our brief time of being family so that the knowledge she received about Jesus prepared her for eternity. More than one life was changed by that unwanted move.

Another move was similar. My mom, in her pain over divorce a few years later, decided that we were going to move somewhere far away from Indiana, so she moved us to New Mexico. I was indignant with her because I was a junior in high school and happy where I was. She invited my sisters and me to help pick out the town where we would live, though I was still hoping not to go. I prayed so hard that God would change her mind, but there was no budging on her part and she would not agree to let me stay behind.

Once the move happened, we found another Methodist church, where my mom became the youth leader. There I was introduced by several friends to the Baptism of the Holy Spirit. Acts refers to two different kinds of baptism, John's baptism and Jesus' baptism (Acts 19:1-7). Eventually I attended another church and that Pastor taught me more about how to listen and follow the Holy Spirit and how to study the Scriptures. These things changed my life immeasurably, as I began to be aware of the Spirit realm and the power of intercession with my prayer language. During this time I was also baptized in water as a sign that I was a believer. God was fathering me and I didn't even recognize it. These experiences of God's amazing redemption came after what seemed to be unanswered prayers.

When I was a young mom with my first child Brooke, another incident caused me to question God's answering my cry for help, until I heard His perspective many months later. One night my husband David was away at a weekend retreat with the men in our church in Dallas. I had put Brooke down in her crib and had gone to bed. As I was just drifting off into sleep, I saw the hall light dim, then brighten, as though someone had walked in front of it. I didn't hear anything, but my entire body went on high alert and my imagination began to go wild. Fear gripped me as I realized I was alone in the house with my baby and it appeared someone else was there too! As the minutes went by, terror took hold of my body and my mind. I was shaking in the bed and, very quickly, the fear hit my stomach. I knew I had to get to the bathroom, but was terrified of alerting the intruder.

Quietly tiptoeing into the bathroom, with my phone in hand, I dialed 911. The operator was as convinced as I that someone was inside my home when she heard the terror in my voice. She instructed me to stay in the bathroom until the police arrived. After what felt like 20 minutes, but was really only half that, there was a loud knock at the front door and I went running down the hall to answer it.

As I approached the front door, my husband David startled me with his sudden appearance from the garage past our kitchen. I literally screamed out loud! As the officers yelled out, "Ma'am, are you ok?", I opened the front door. I was in complete confusion as to why David was home from out of town, and, in my surprise and fear, I wasn't able to fully process what was happening.

My scream of shock was so authentic, that the officers quizzed me several times with, "Are you sure this is your husband?". Finally I convinced them he truly was my husband. David's story tumbled out that he'd returned home unexpectedly from out of town. He didn't want to wake me, so he crept down the hall to check on the baby and then returned to the garage where there was a couch.

Today this story has a component of hilarity to it, but at the time it was terrifying. Our imagination is so powerful. I thought there was an intruder and my mind filled in the frightening details!

For the next approximately nine months I was visited over and over again in the night by a demonic being that would stand beside our bed at my feet. I would awaken to sense this very tall, dark, shadowy being. I tried valiantly to fight it and make it go away. Initially, I had to awaken David and have him pray, as I was completely frozen by fear. Slowly I began to be able to say scriptures on my own, and eventually I was able to command the demon to go and it would leave. However, it took months for me to reach this level of faith. I became so frustrated with myself and with my lack of faith! I didn't understand why the demon would keep coming back and why I couldn't get it to leave permanently. I felt that I was either doing something wrong or God was not answering. The torment finally ended when I didn't react to the demon's occasional presence.

About a year later, I was talking to God about the excruciating process I'd been through and asked why it had happened. He replied, "This was training for your future." I was surprised by His answer but it brought peace to me, even though I had no grid for what He meant at the time. I didn't know that He was going to bring me oppressed individuals who needed someone with authority and confidence to address the demonic realm that was oppressing them. I had no idea at that time that I would eventually work with people who had violence and intense trauma in their backgrounds. It was many years before I fully understood that there was a purpose in the struggle I went through. God never wastes anything in our journey if we let Him transform it for His glory. He transforms our places of weakness into places of strength. His word says that He makes even the valley of weeping a place of streams.[36]

Feeling "hidden away" in my ministry has also caused me to question if the Father was answering my prayers. I have been told over and over that I should be speaking more. I receive confirmation every time I speak and I watch the Holy Spirit "connect the dots" for people as I share from the platform. Yet no matter how many positive reviews come, and despite my many prayers for more open doors, the offers to speak are few and infrequent.

I have always wondered why God didn't answer these prayers for more opportunities to speak. Then I had an encounter that convinced me to stop praying that prayer. I pulled up in my driveway at my landlord's home one day, and was about to exit the car when I saw a tall hooded figure in a grey sweatshirt standing behind my vehicle. I was startled and was contemplating staying in the car for safety, but as I asked the Lord if it was safe, I felt His peace.

I got out and turned around to greet the person. The individual was really tall and I initially thought it was a man, but it turned out to be a woman. She approached slowly and asked if I lived in this house and worked in the basement. All the while I was wondering, "Why in the world is she asking me this?" She proceeded to say that she had a word for me that she'd received while prayer-walking our neighborhood! I told her I was happy to hear what she had to share.

The woman told me that the Lord had told her that I was a secret weapon in His hand, and that the work I did in the basement was kept hidden from the enemy. She continued to speak, saying that I was affecting the Kingdom of Light with what I did. I almost started laughing, as I confirmed to her that I did indeed live in the basement and that I worked with people to overcome trauma and abuse. I was filled with joy and hope because of her words. They brought powerful encouragement to my heart that the Father knew exactly what I was

---

[36]*The Holy Bible, New Living Translation,* Psalm 86:6 (Carol Stream, IL: Tyndale House Publishing, 2015).

doing and He was accomplishing great things through our partnership together. It settled that question of "why" profoundly for me. My confidence is not based on the world's view of success but on my obedience to do what He shows me to do. It is my joy to honor Him in the process. Again, God had a different perspective from mine. I had believed that I must be doing something wrong because my ministry wasn't out front, but all the time God was keeping me hidden to increase my effectiveness for His purposes.

Pursuing the Presence, the instrumental CD that David and I recorded the summer before his cancer diagnosis, was another life circumstance where God brought further enlightenment about both unanswered prayers and His provision. David and I had felt the leading of the Holy Spirit to record a spontaneous, or improvisational, music CD to encourage meditation and prayer. We prayed into this project for over five years and still didn't have the connections or funds to make the recording. I kept sensing from the Holy Spirit that there was a specific window of time for this project, and the impression increased as the year of 2001 approached.

At a conference we were attending in the fall, a man approached us to ask if we'd ever wanted to undertake a recording project. We responded with a resounding yes! We continued telling him that we felt it was to be a spontaneous recording. The man, Jeff, enthusiastically offered us his studio for this purpose free of charge. His one qualifier was that he had to first finish building his studio in Dallas.

We waited for several months, then the following spring we got the call that he was ready for us. We hopped on a plane and arrived at his home only to find that the studio was still not operational. What a big surprise! Normally I would have freaked out, but this time I felt the Lord's tangible peace and so did David. It was so bizarre to feel peace in the midst of what looked like chaos. We decided that we would rest in what the Holy Spirit was giving us and wait and see what happened. In the meantime, we helped Jeff run cables, and hang doors, and whatever else we could do to accelerate the completion of the studio. We had planned for less than a week there. The day before we were to fly home, Jeff announced that the musicians were arriving that night to record. Mind you, we had never met these musicians--- a bass player, a prophetic drum team, and a guitarist --- but Jeff assured us they were the right people for the adventure! He had also invited several folks to pray on site as we recorded.

That evening as we gathered to give the instructions ---"Here is the key we are starting in. Here is the picture we want to paint"--- we were filled with nervous anticipation. We were finally here but would what we had believed for actually happen?

The first attempt ended, and with a heavy heart, I came out of my sound booth commenting that it didn't go very well, and saying we probably would have to do another take. Jeff, however, was shaking his head in amazement and contradicting my disappointment with his excitement, saying it was incredible. We all sat together in front of the soundboard and listened to the playback. I was completely astonished, as we all heard the beauty and wonder of the song that David eventually titled, "The Awakening". The breath of the Spirit was on it and the waves of sound felt like water washing our spirits as we listened. We recorded the next four opuses in a few hours, only having to do two takes on one song.[37] The voice of the Lord truly sang through our instruments.

I only had one concern. I had been having a thought since we'd arrived in Dallas, that one of the tracks was going to disappear. Jeff assured me that such an accident was impossible. He had the latest and greatest multi-layered recording technology, with all kinds of back ups. Nevertheless, we prayed and committed it all to the Lord and asked for His divine protection. However, we would soon find out my premonition was valid, and when my thoughts became a reality, it appeared our prayers for covering and provision were not answered.

David and I said our goodbyes to Jeff as he began the mix the next day. We arrived back home and began to settle back into normal life, remembering and basking in our supernatural experience with the

---

[37] David and Laurie Morris, *Pursuing the Presence* (iTunes, 2001).

recording. Several days later we received a phone call from Jeff. He had been up for two days and nights trying to restore a flute track of mine that had disappeared! He couldn't believe this had happened! He'd finally resigned himself to it being gone for good and was calling to tell me I had to fly back and re-record the final track of the CD, "The Throne."

I was irrationally upset, and began crying because I felt so angry and afraid. How could God let this happen? Why would He let this happen? After my hissy fit was over, David tried to encourage me that I could practice with the track and it would help with the new recording. I was opposed to this, as it would not be demonstrating integrity if we were saying this was a spontaneous recording. I also knew my mind would get in the way of my following the Spirit's flow if I practiced.

David was so confident that I had been born to do this, but I was scared. Though I kept trying to come into agreement with his faith, I was irritated at being put in such a challenging position. I finally agreed to go back to Jeff's and re-record my flute track and booked my flight for the following week.

After arriving at the studio, Jeff and I prayed and he encouraged me with his faith in my ability to follow the Holy Spirit's nuance. As Jeff set up my headphones and set new levels, I was not full of faith. I weakly asked Jesus for help and the recording began. It was over in a few short minutes, and my first response was similar to the one I'd had on the night of our initial recording. "We are going to have to do it again!" to which Jeff responded by shaking his head, and saying it was better than the first recording.

When we listened to the playback I was amazed at the beauty and synchronization of my playing with the pre-recorded track. Again, only God could empower me to do what seemed impossible. I have referred to this event as the most supernatural experience of my walk with God as I can take absolutely no credit for what occurred on that album except for me showing up! What had seemed to be "unanswered prayer", the Lord used to challenge me to trust Him and to increase my faith in His power. In addition, He made the next recording even more beautiful than the original.

I will share one last one story that involved waiting for 20 years before receiving a sudden breakthrough two years ago. I don't fully understand why it took the length of time it did. However, I believe that cumulative personal prayer and corporate prayer converged and brought a shift of sizable proportions in my daughter Brynne's life. Just as many Bible saints had to wait for their promises, so we waited for the key to healing for Brynne as she suffered through an assault on her health and wellness. I'll explain as best as I can.

When Brynne was an infant, there was a man on staff at our church who was very charismatic and spiritually gifted. He was charming and favored because he moved in supernatural gifts. He had come from a family positioned high up in witchcraft and the occult. He'd been saved into the Kingdom of Light, but we came to realize that this man was still operating out of darkness. He was living a double life. He presented himself as a godly pastor while hurting young men sexually. As a church, we ended up turning him over to the police for prosecution for the crimes he committed.

In her growing up years, Brynne had constant accidents, injuries and illnesses that seemed to grow worse the older she got. As we kept calling out to God for healing and protection and for the key to why this was such a pattern, I kept remembering a day when the aforementioned pastor was holding Brynne for me while I ministered to a family member in crisis. As he held her that day he had prayed over her and I had always had a funny feeling that somehow something wasn't quite right. When this memory would come up, I would often discount it, as I had no tangible proof to back up what I sensed. I didn't connect that the Holy Spirit was highlighting this memory because it was a key for Brynne's freedom.

Fast forward many years. I eventually began working with a client from that area, who brought to light that they had been prayed over and set apart by the same man mentioned above, when they were very young. He had "marked" them for the purpose of being used by the occult. A knowing sense flooded me that this guy had marked Brynne in prayer as an infant as well. This marking was the same thing as a curse. I concluded that the multitude of illnesses and accidents were the result of this man's curse on my daughter. We immediately broke this curse off in prayer, and were hopeful that something had shifted, but though there was a lessening of physical accidents, there still seemed to still be a vulnerability.

A few years later, Brynne experienced a serious shoulder injury that required surgery. She was in physical therapy in preparation for this, when we had a church-wide retreat with our fellowship. One night during the retreat, a leader called Brynne out for prayer for her healing. As people began to pray over her someone shared a picture God had given them of sharks circling around Brynne. I immediately felt it had to do with that curse, and that it still had some hold on her. People began walking around her, circling and declaring her wholeness and healing. After about ten minutes of warring and worshipping, Brynne began to excitedly raise her arm, something she'd not been able to do before, and declared she was healed! Her Physical Therapist happened to be with us that night and confirmed that there had been a bonafide healing! This was validated by the Doctor soon after this.

I knew that I knew that something had shifted in the spirit realm, and that the healing we had cried out for these 20 years had finally occurred. The curse set in place all those years ago was fully broken. The corporate agreement was what we had always needed. Brynne and I knew it was done and the fruit in her health since that time has been tangible proof. She has had very few minor injuries since that time several years ago. The breakthrough for which we pounded heaven had finally come. Waiting produces patience and is intended by God to strengthen our faith.

We don't always understand the Father's ways, but we can trust that He is always working out a blessing for us, whatever we're facing. Whether He is working our faith muscles again to trust His provision, or teaching us to have empathy and not judgment towards others, there is something good to come from every circumstance when we "invite" Him to work. God is the one in charge of our lives.

I have experienced many humbling things that have awakened compassion and taught me to give grace to others who are in difficult or confounding circumstances. For instance, in the past I would sometimes secretly and self-righteously look down on those with financial issues, believing they were guilty of not being good stewards, but my own challenges in this area broke my judgmental attitude. God is always wanting to conform our hearts to His, to bring a holy perspective.

Perspective is the key word here. When it appears God hasn't come through for us, we tend to think that He doesn't love us or hasn't heard us. Our limited view of this life and our circumstances can't compare to God's birds-eye view from eternity. We often expect or demand for our felt needs to be met according to our timetable. However, God's ways, even when they don't make sense to us, draw us into dependence on Him. He is whispering, "Will You trust that I have your good in mind in every way?". His purposes are being accomplished, no matter the circumstances. We will experience His peace and walk in His grace even when we don't understand if we will put our faith in Who He is and trust Him to do what is best. Romans 11: 33-36 says it like this: "Oh, the depth of the riches and wisdom and knowledge of God! How unsearchable are His judgments and decisions. How unfathomable and untraceable are His ways! For who has known the mind of the Lord and who has been His counselor?"[38] Let us be some of the faithful followers mentioned in Hebrews 11 who do not waiver in waiting for our promises to be fulfilled and who trust in Who He is!

I'm reminded of Abraham's waiting for 15 years for the promise of a child, and then another 10 years went by after God's reassurance that He was going to fulfill what He said. I don't think there is much for which I have actively waited in faith for that long. I am also reminded of a prayer journey David and I took with Dutch Sheets in the '90's.

---

[38]*Amplified Holy Bible*, Romans 11:33-36.

We sowed in prayer and worship in the Cathedrals of England, asking for a move of God among the British people. We traveled around the country, prayer-walking and holding celebrations of prayer and worship in these beautiful historic places of faith. We were praying for revival in the churches there, for spiritual awakening, for salvations, and for unity in the Body of Christ. All these years since, those who went on our team have not known for what fruit was born from that time of intercession and worship. Then recently I was told that Pete Greig of the 24/7 Prayer Network is leading a prayer initiative throughout England. Some of their corporate gatherings of worship and celebration will be in the same churches and Cathedrals that we visited all over England. My spirit leapt inside, feeling that this was related to our pioneering alongside others in prayer years before. The fruit is just beginning.

We have a choice whether to live with mindsets like, "God isn't for me", "I'm not as good as everyone else", and "He doesn't answer my prayers," or "I can't trust Him". These mindsets are actually those of a victim and were birthed in our negative experiences. Cumulative trauma, pain, and loss set us up in our hearts and minds to agree with these thoughts. The vulnerability that comes from painful trauma makes us susceptible to negative expectations. With the Holy Spirit's healing and help, we can align our mind and heart with the reality that we are sons and daughters of the Most High God who loves us and is working out the hard and ugly things into something beautiful and redemptive. His love is so deep and so wide that He made provision before time for His son Jesus to become a man, to atone for our sins, and to bring victory over death and the grave. Whether we always see answered prayers or not, His question to me and to you again and again is, "Will you love me for who I am and not just for what I do? I've already provided in my Son all that you need. Is it not enough?"

In today's culture there are many things that challenge the goodness and faithfulness of God. One of the more serious challenges is that so many in this generation do not believe that the Word of God as found in the scriptures is inerrant. God's Word is alive and active and powerful according to Hebrews 4:12. Will you resolve in your heart to settle the issue that God's Word and His name can be trusted implicitly?

Lord give me eyes to see like You do. Give me a heart that trusts when I don't understand. Help me remember that You live and move outside of time of space. You are eternal and my perspective is finite. I lean into the truth that You are altogether good, altogether faithful, and You cannot lie! Give me eyes of faith and a heart that trusts in Who You Are and not merely in what I see! Cause my faith to rest in Your Word and in Who You are...a faithful God.

My final resolve is to trust You
To believe all that You do is for my good
And when I don't understand, I will say it again
You are faithful and true to Your word

My Trust is in You Lord
My Hope is in believing Your plans for me
My Strength is in You Lord - My life is in Your hands

You're my Rock and my Shield and my Fortress
I depend upon the safety of Your love
And when the enemy comes, into Your name I will run
For I'm safe beneath the power of Your blood

My Trust is in You Lord
My Hope is in believing Your plans for me
My Strength is in You Lord - My Life is in Your hands

David Morris ©1998

Chapter 5: Injustice: Trusting God's Redemption

Like many of you reading my story, I have suffered through many injustices. Some of those painful events were big, like my late husband's infidelities, and some of them were small, like a friend failing on a commitment. One of my bigger betrayals I did not share in my first book because it wasn't brought to closure at the time. As of 2019, however, it has come full circle and I felt it was important to include it here.

One day at work in 2006, when I was living in Collinsville, Illinois, I received a very strange phone call. The caller said, "Hello, this is Tony with the FDA branch of the FBI. I would like to speak with you about someone we are investigating." I immediately thought the call was a prank from one of my younger friends David, or David's brother Dallas. They all loved to prank me.

I laughed and replied, "Ok, Dallas, give it up." The interchange continued with the gentleman insisting he was with the FBI. I continued the banter, but the guy was not laughing. Imagine my mortification when I asked him to fax me his badge to prove he was who he claimed to be, and then receiving the fax with an actual FBI badge staring at me from the page!

I pulled myself together and asked him what this call was in reference to. He replied, "Dr. Christine Daniel". My heart dropped to the bottom of my stomach. Dr. Daniel was the doctor who had treated David while he was fighting his cancer in 2002 in Los Angeles at her private clinic. My mind began racing and my heart began pounding as I tried to imagine why the FBI would be calling me about her so many years after David's passing.

The phone conversation with the FBI agent was both shocking and unbelievable to me. The agent said that the FBI had been trying to track me down for over a year. He said there were no records of our having been at Dr. Daniel's clinic. I couldn't believe it! This was such a lie! We had been at the clinic from the end of January 2002 through the second week of May that year, receiving Dr. Daniel's holistic treatments and prayer for David's cancer. We had spent $75,000 dollars for his treatments and I had boxes of receipts to prove it. I was so confused and baffled.

The agent gently explained more of the story. The FBI wanted to prosecute Dr. Daniel for manslaughter but couldn't because all the patients who had ever been at the clinic had died. In addition, there were no family members left who had spent enough time with Dr. Daniel to give reliable, eyewitness testimony. The prosecutor determined that the best way to bring her to justice was to indict her for fraud for making false claims of healing cancer. They also wanted to prosecute her for tax evasion related to the money she collected in fees.

I had a hard time taking in what the agent was saying. I was at war inside trying to reconcile the things the agent was telling me with my belief that Dr. Daniel was a believer and loved Jesus. I initially felt there was no way she would have committed such a crime. Her faith was one of the reasons we had gone to her clinic in the first place. In addition, there had been personal testimonies of healing from people at the clinic that we knew personally.

But I was also reminded of some things that felt "off" or "weird" in my interactions with her and the office staff, things that happened during the intense battle for David's life. I was traveling back and forth across the United States between my home in North Carolina and the clinic in California, caring for my kids, and caring for David. I was also driving David to the clinic each day from the place where we were staying in Camarillo, California. There was simply no time or energy to process the doubts that arose about the clinic. Those days were highly stressful for our whole family, especially being apart from our children so much. Brooke, our oldest at the time was having to hold down the fort and care for her siblings and support their home schooling, which was a heavy burden for her. To find out that those sacrifices we made might have been worthless was devastating!

That day the agent asked for my help gathering specific documents that proved we had paid the clinic for treatment for David's cancer. He was kind and empathetic, saying that their team understood that to dig through old stuff was painful, but he also stated that I was the first person that they had contacted who had pictures and receipts proving they had been at the clinic. He assured me that he would give me time to think about it and decide whether I felt up to helping them.

At first, I felt there was no way I could help the FBI in its investigation. I had just decided to move back to North Carolina from Illinois. I was packing up the house and trying to sell it. In addition, I had been dating a man and had finally decided he was not the man God had for me. The FBI request seemed to be just another emotional weight, so I said no.

The agent persisted over the next couple of weeks with his request. During one of his phone calls, he shared more painful and difficult information about Dr. Daniel's lack of integrity that shocked me and caused me to question my initial decision. In the search and seizure of the doctor's home, they had confiscated products she had been making for her patients. Testing of those products revealed sunscreen in some of them! I couldn't wrap my mind around this. She had told me those products were raw, unfiltered chemo that she had to import from

73

another country. I was horrified that she would do that to another human being! How could a believer and a medical doctor lie to us?

Over the next few days I remembered a conversation I had with the daughter of someone else who had died at the clinic. The woman had shared with me that an autopsy showed that her mom had all kinds of sludge in her kidneys and that she'd actually had renal failure as her cause of death. The Coroner hadn't identified the sludge, but my friend thought it was weird. I then connected the dots. David's autopsy had said the same thing. His cause of death was listed as renal failure and there was undetermined sludge in his kidneys. I could not prove it, but knew in my gut that the sludge was likely related to the sunscreen.

Once the agent told me about the sunscreen, I felt I had to find the documents they needed. I asked my oldest daughter to help me go through the boxes of receipts and pictures from our time at the clinic. There was a deadline for finding the information the FBI needed, so I had no time to even begin to process my emotions or evaluate my fresh need to forgive. The FBI also said that I would be called on eventually to testify before the Grand Jury. I never dreamed it would be seven years before there was full resolution on the matter.

Dr. Daniel's betrayal meant that I had to face another level of grief with my family as we looked at the incredible injustice that had been done to so many families who were in the same painful circumstances as ours. Most of the other families had lost everything financially to send their loved ones to the clinic. They were duped, just as we were, by testimonies of healing and by the offer of help with a faith-focused protocol.

God had blessed us through the giving of thousands of people who contributed to the costs of David's treatment. I've been told that we may be the only family not devastated financially by the scam. I will be eternally grateful to those people who gave and to God for covering us. The fact that we were saved when others were not, activated in me some "survivors guilt" for a period of time, until I accepted that I would never know why things happened the way they did, but the fact remained that we had been protected, and I was grateful. The only thing the Father said to me during that season of provision was, "For such time as this." David and I had always given faithfully over and above a tithe to the local church, and this felt like a cumulative return on that giving at just the right time. People since then have asked if there will be any financial restitution to the families, but unfortunately, no money was ever found to recompense anyone.

The process of trial preparation, the trial itself, and the verdict took seven long years. I was not subpoenaed to testify before the Grand Jury until late spring of 2011, right before I was moving to Kansas City. A dedicated prosecutor, Joseph Johns, and his team, fought hard during those years to bring Dr. Daniel to justice. In the end, her medical license was revoked, she was forbidden to practice medicine in the area hospitals, and eventually she was sentenced to prison in 2013.

The trial itself was intimidating and emotionally hard as I faced the woman who had lied and stolen from me. The last time I had seen her was to tell her I was taking David home, and her response had been horribly accusatory. She declared that if I took him from her clinic, he would die. As I took the stand, I took a deep breath, and asked for the Holy Spirit's peace and recall. I was the number two witness and a lot was riding my testimony and that of my deceased friend's husband. We had each been on site at the clinic for longer periods of time while the rest of the witnesses had only visited for brief times during their loved ones' treatment there. Because I had stayed in California for weeks at a time, my testimony of what I'd seen first hand was important.

As the cross examination began by the defense, I felt shaky and scared. The defense attorney was intense and aggressive and even inferred I was lying on the stand. But in the midst of the cross examination, my fear began to dissipate and my voice became steady. I felt the strength of the Holy Spirit rise up and I felt the fight in me rise to defend the truth. I had nothing to be afraid of. It was a precious gift from God to get to confront her, and it brought concrete closure to such a difficult betrayal. As I left the stand, I was shaking, and I started crying as soon as I was in a room alone for debriefing. Adrenaline was coursing through my body, but I could also feel the relief and peace of the Lord now that it was over. I had stood up and confronted the woman who had stolen so much from so many.

When the trial finally ended two years later, due to several postponements, I couldn't even tell you the length of her sentence. My kids and I were invited to come to the sentencing, but all of us felt that chapter of our lives was over and chose not to go. We did write the Judge and asked him to consider the great loss of life and betrayal that occurred through Dr. Daniel when he sentenced her.

So how did I let it go? I chose, even before testifying, to forgive her and her family. Several family members were working incognito at the clinic without our knowledge. I resolved in my heart to rest in the word the Father gave me in Isaiah 57:1-2: The righteous man perishes and no one takes it to heart; Faithful and devout men are taken away while no one understands that the righteous person is taken away from disaster and evil. He enters into peace; they rest in their beds, each one who walked uprightly.[39] I knew it was not Dr. Daniel that took David. It was not her lying or her fake medicine or her feigned healing power that took his life. David had needed a miracle no matter what; the cancer that attacked his body was deadly. Eventually I wrote Dr. Daniel a letter confronting what she had done, and acknowledging and releasing my pain and forgiveness towards her.

It is important to remember that forgiveness is not saying what a person did to offend us is OK; rather, forgiveness is releasing that person into the hands of a just God who has already paid the penalty for their sin and ours. How did I know I was healed and free and that I'd really let it go? I experienced the fruit of forgiveness: freedom from harassing thoughts, the ability to pray for her, peace, and not living with the question of what if, and knowing that I had grieved through the pain.

When we are harboring unforgiveness we may experience unpleasant symptoms: anger, depression, passivity, staying busy, turning to addictions, being super-sensitive and easily triggered,

---

[39].*Amplified Holy Bible,* Isaiah 57:1-2.

derision, sickness in the body. Unforgiveness will always "leak out" in some way in our lives.

Forgiveness is commonly not just a one-and-done statement. Most of the time, forgiveness involves being specific and can take several times of choosing to let someone or something go. Why does it often take more than one time of forgiving? These are a few of the common reasons:

Our pride and entitlement that feels its more than others have endured;

Sometimes we don't want to remember so we can't see it all to let go of it;

Somehow we feel the unforgiveness keeps us safe or strong.

It is essential that we choose to forgive, and it is essential that we allow ourselves to grieve the pain and hurt. I call this place of release "holy alignment," and it brings a shift in our emotions and mindsets. When we forgive, God forgives us and the reality of the Cross applies.

Choosing to forgive doesn't mean that we have to engage in deep relationship again with every person who has hurt us! Some forgiveness leads to an ongoing and fully restored relationship with the individual who hurt us, but not always. In other words, not all forgiveness is demonstrated or played out in our relationships the same way. Sometimes we forgive but we hold a boundary that we will not be in close relationship with that person.

For example, when I chose to forgive some of the men that my late husband had slept with, there were some decided differences in what that looked like after my initial step of choosing to forgive. The Father told me to contact one of the men after David died. I shared with him that I knew of his encounters and that I forgave him. He wept and received grace to forgive himself from my extending forgiveness. If I saw this man today, I would feel nothing but love and grace for him. With another man, however --- someone who had been in a close mentoring relationship with us but never owned his sin --- the Father directed me to forgive him through a phone call, but to maintain a boundary of no relationship with him. If I saw him today, I would not feel ill will, but I would be cautious with trusting him because he's not demonstrated a repentant heart or a changed lifestyle.

As believers, one of the most common areas of unforgiveness I run across is towards God Himself. Because we know He is perfect, we often don't own our judgments of Him. We rationalize our anger, disappointment and mistrust with Him and don't actually acknowledge it and let it go. This is so important! David in the Psalms acknowledged His judgments frequently.

I also have come to believe that when we forgive, we are aiding wounds in being healed and restoration ripples out to the relationships around us, bringing release in various ways. I've witnessed a few stunning shifts in clients' behavior and relationships after they released forgiveness. One example was a couple I was working with forgave their son and it was the catalyst for their son coming back into their lives the same week they forgave, after avoiding them for years. I experienced a profound shift with my oldest daughter when she was about eight. When I forgave my mom at a deeper heart level than in the past, Brooke shared some things that she never had the day after I forgave. I've seen circumstances change like this with hundreds and hundreds of clients through the years. We end up benefiting with freedom when we release our forgiveness!

The hardest thing to forgive surrounding Dr. Daniel's betrayal was the loss of time for David and me with our kids as a family. The community support we would have had if we had been at a hospital closer to home was another painful loss. The fact that generous people had given to something that wasn't real broke my heart. Eventually I heard the Lord say, "They gave in faith and I always honor that. They sowed so they will reap." All of these losses I had to process over time. I regularly share when I'm teaching that God is a God of specifics, and forgiving specifically for the different ways we are hurt or betrayed is powerful.

When we left the clinic, I focused on getting David home in time to say good-bye to his children. We were both still believing for his miracle, but time with our family and friends was so important. After being home for two days, David lost lucidity. One evening the Holy Spirit said to gather the kids and to "say goodbye without saying goodbye." Unsure of what that meant, I followed through and gathered the kids around David. He had not been present mentally the entire day, but when I asked him if he could bless the kids, he immediately responded, although weakly, and laid his hand on each of them, speaking a blessing and calling them by name. What a gift of closure. He went to be with Jesus the next morning right after speaking to his mom very briefly.

Why didn't I share any of this earlier? Back in 2007 when I wrote my first book, the trial had not happened and was not even in sight; there was no assurance that justice would be served. I felt that my sharing this part of the journey could have injured those who supported David and me, particularly those who contributed to send David to the clinic. I felt it was time to share this story now, over seventeen years since David's passing, for two reasons: one, my sharing now could serve as a warning and bring awareness that there are wolves in sheep's clothing in the world who seek to harm God's people; and two, our experience can encourage all of us to discern and research things that are presented to us, even businesses and ministries run by believers. The invitation to go there initially was through a friend, which added to our vulnerability and blind trust. Naiveté is dangerous! I did the best research I could in the short amount of time I had to help David. Sadly, it wasn't enough. Though she was a licensed medical professional, Dr. Daniel was a liar and a charlatan. There appeared to be a few miracles at her clinic, but the "healings" were from a placebo effect at best and didn't last.

The other reason I've shared the whole story is because I just finished filming with the Oxygen Network for a DocuSeries called *License to Kill* that was released in June 2019. The network approached me in 2018, asking me to be interviewed about our experience with Dr. Daniel and what happened after we left the clinic. Tim, my new husband, and I prayed with a few others for several weeks about whether to do the interview. I wanted to participate if it would help others and bring hope to those who have suffered injustice, but I was leery of focusing on Dr. Daniel. I had closed the door on that season, and I know that she is paying her penalty. After prayer for several weeks, I felt led to do the project and ended up flying out to Los Angeles in September of 2018 to do the taping.

As much as I had chosen to forgive and move on, reviewing the details of that painful time dredged up all kinds of fresh emotions and grief. Layers of forgiveness can sometimes be years apart. I referred earlier to the analogy of the onion, layers related to our emotions, and some emotions buried in our subconscious. Even when we have deliberately worked through our grief, times of mourning may continue to surface periodically through the years. Grief is reactivated or uncovered as we experience new painful circumstances or momentous events that remind us of what was lost or stolen. The difference in my grief most recently was that it didn't feel debilitating, although it felt very deep. It didn't shut me down. I was able to grieve intensely for a few days and process my regrets, remember, and then let the pain go. We can look back and assess what we might have done differently, learn and possibly understand more as time goes on. However, we can't ever change the past, so it isn't constructive to ask "what if" or to wish "I should have". As my friend Lorrie says, "woulda's and shoulda's have to be dropped! There is no grace in the past or in the future; grace is given each day."

Many of us have experienced injustice at the hands of others, sometimes even from leaders in the Church or from people in authority whom we trusted. I attended a conference recently given by well-known psychologist and speaker, Diane Langburg. She reiterated how devastating the betrayal of leaders in the church can be. "The leadership of the Body of Christ has misused power to abuse or victimize in a myriad of ways, and statistics are on the high end."[40] In

---

[40] Diane Langburg, *The Church as a Refuge*, Conference held at Colonial Presbyterian Church, Kansas City, MO, April 19, 2018.

Emotionally Healthy Spirituality, Pete Scazzaro says, "Christian spirituality, without an integration of emotional health, can be deadly—to yourself, your relationship with God, and the people around you.[41]

I personally have experienced inappropriate control and accusation, other than the duplicity of Dr. Daniel, at various times in my walk with the Lord. These leaders were not horrible people; in fact, they were people I respected, making it particularly hard to understand. In each situation, I had a personal relationship with these individuals, and yet they did or said things that hurt me and broke trust. These leaders were wounded, just like we all are. They operated out of their own brokenness and imprints, with fear and in a controlling manner. I heard someone say once that the most controlling people are the most shame-based people. Fear and shame lead to us to try to control our world and others. To an individual who has been injured, and is walking alone, without a support system of healthy relationships, or without having the accountability of a board and oversight, this is a setup for isolation and a difficult road to healing. I have met many hurting individuals who have never entered into intimate relationships in the Church again, after being wounded by a leader. The pain of betrayal was just too much for them to process alone. We need each other, and especially when we are hurting and vulnerable!

One of the reasons I believe I've had the capacity to forgive and trust again is that I have been privileged to have safe, mature people to walk in accountable and supportive relationship with me. I've also been careful who I've invited into those emotional vulnerable places. There have been different people at different seasons, but they have helped me process and given me insight into the bigger picture whenever conflict or accusation arose. I determined to be as open to correction as I could be, knowing that my heart could be deceitful and my perspective might not always be completely accurate. Therefore I prayerfully and vulnerably submitted to those around me who had wisdom and knew me well enough to confront any blind spots in me.

---

[41] Peter Scazzero, *Emotionally Healthy Spirituality,*), p. 9.

One of my more painful situations involved someone in authority over me who cornered me and said things they had no right to say to me. This person disagreed with some of my personal choices, not a choice that was unethical or unbiblical but more a matter of differing opinions, and they confronted me in a violating way, raising their voice, and making accusing statements about my character. They not only did this without warning but in front of other people. They never repented for this to me, but the Lord prompted someone in authority over this leader to call me on the very day this event took place. They prayed over me, validated my pain, and gave me counsel on how to proceed with my relationship with this person. They helped me sort through all the things that were said. I didn't want to ignore anything I needed to own myself, but I also didn't want to let their judgments take root and damage my heart. In this case, there wasn't much truth in what they said, but often when others accuse us of something there can be a grain or nugget of truth to be considered, especially if it's a pattern of a similar accusation.

In another situation, the disagreement was not resolved quickly or easily. The scripture says we should be at peace with all men as much as it's in our power to do so.[42] Therefore, it was worth it to wade through the awkward conversations and confrontations in order to preserve the relationship. My ownership of any part I had played in this conflict was important for me and for the other party. It is so important in the hard places of our lives to continually be open to the Holy Spirit's correction and to get insight from those around us. Please know that I am not referring to social networking communities but to intimate, live relationships! We are not designed to go it alone. We need the Body of Christ for support, prayer, insight, and perspective. We should open ourselves to people we can trust for challenge, accountability, and correction, not just for validation and comfort.

---

[42] *New American Standard Bible*, Romans 12:18 (Anaheim, California: The Lockman Foundation, Copyright 1960, 1962, 1963, 1968, 1971, 1972), Used by permission.

Whatever you have faced or are facing that feels unjust, run to the Father and ask for His justice and His way to be done. Forgive at all costs. Hebrews 12:15 says not to let a root of bitterness spring up within you or it can defile you and others. Guard your heart and don't give the enemy a foothold.[43] Let it go --- whether or not the one who has offended you apologizes or repents --- let it go. Whether we see justice here on earth or not, His justice will prevail according to Romans 12:19: "Beloved, never avenge yourselves, but leave the way open for God's wrath and His judicial righteousness."[44] Remember that justice is not always measurable in our eyes, but God always has just balances.

Holy Spirit, give me the grace to keep my eyes on You and to remember that You are a God who will recompense and bring justice --- whether I see it in this lifetime or not. Please give me patience. Help me to cultivate joy in waiting for Your hand to move. I release and forgive anyone who has unintentionally or intentionally betrayed me. I give them to You for Your righteous mercy and judgment. Help me remember that we are all broken and in need of forgiveness. Father, Your ways are not my ways, and I know that I may never understand You fully. Bring Your holy perspective on the events I do not understand. I choose to trust You as the perfect Judge and the One who knows every heart. Give me courage when I need to speak up and confront. Remind me that I have a voice. Thank you for having mercy on me in my own sin. Keep me walking in the light and in forgiveness.

This song came a few years ago as I looked at all the loss and trauma in my journey, yet remembered the goodness of our God and the real end game of this journey here on earth. Let us remember the

---

[43] *New American Standard Bible*, Hebrews 12:1.
[44] *Amplified Holy Bible*, Romans 12:19.

heroes of the faith in Hebrews 11 who set their faith like a rock, even though some did not see the promises fulfilled in this life.

This life is not the real deal, It's just a breath
Eternity is more real, so hard to comprehend
We look towards our inheritance, life evermore
Living in His presence, our great reward

We fix our eyes on You, Author of our faith
Enduring for our sake, help us run this race
We fix our eyes on You, Anchor of our souls
Enduring for our sake, help us reach the goal!
This life is not the real deal, it's just a breath
Eternity is more real, so hard to understand
Our hearts are drawn towards heaven, and those who've gone before
Holding onto Your promises and the life we're longing for!

We fix our eyes on You, Author of our faith
Enduring for our sake, help us run this race
We fix our eyes on You, Anchor of our souls
Enduring for our sake, help us reach the goal!

You give us what we need
You are Who You say You are
Always kind and just
Redeeming all things for our good
So when life is hard we stand in what You've done
When sorrow comes, we know You're here with us
So we look to You, Jesus, we look to You, Jesus.

Laurie M Goddu ©

Chapter 6: Waiting for my Isaac

Shortly after David passed, I had a dear friend say to me something along the lines of, "You know, statistically, if you aren't remarried in the first two years after losing your mate you won't get married for another ten." She didn't mean to hurt me, but the information was not encouraging or comforting. It tore down my faith and hope. It made me feel helpless and as though I was supposed to make something happen. Something I could not and did not want to do. I knew I needed more healing in regards to trusting another man, but I still wanted remarriage and partnership. Another friend said to me, "You'll never find another David," and I retorted, "I don't want another David! I want someone completely different from him."

Because I had honored my husband and deeply loved him, the unhappiness and struggle that were part of our marriage were not something I shared openly. Though he was one of a kind in his personality, and his gifts, the reality was that he wasn't a safe and steady guy for me in our marriage. I didn't want that dynamic in another relationship. I had shut down a part of my heart to David that was never restored. Even before he died he knew this and it hurt his heart. I wanted to be completely open to him, but I just couldn't be the vulnerable, trusting young woman I'd been in the beginning. There were too many broken promises that occurred at crucial times of healing that kept me from fully trusting him. I loved him but didn't fully trust him any longer with all of my heart. Please don't misunderstand; my love for David was deep and rich and I appreciated and respected the unique man he was. God extended immeasurable grace and capacity for us both to heal, but that did not mean I wanted another husband who didn't know who he was, and hadn't been healed of his stuff. If I was to marry again, I needed and wanted someone who was not intimidated by me in any way, and who was whole enough to live out integrity and consistency in our covenant.

For those of you who have lived through, or are living through, betrayal by a spouse or someone else, you know that it takes time to learn to trust them and it takes time to open your heart to them again. Learning to trust my husband was a process for me. The trust had been broken between us in more than one area. My late husband wasn't able to explain several of his insecurities towards me until the year before he died, so I lived for most of our 21 year marriage with questions about some of the ways he interacted with me. (For more understanding of the broken ways of our marriage, read *Shattered, and Then...*)

One night we were sitting in our car, parked in front of our pastor's house, getting ready to meet them for dinner. I once again asked the question that I had asked several times throughout the years, "Why won't you train me as a worship leader? You train other women, but not me. Is it that I'm that bad?" The silence was deafening for several minutes, but then he turned to me and shared something he never had before. "Because I was afraid you'd be better than me. I'm only good at a few things and you are great at so many things. I wanted the worship leading to be just mine." My jaw dropped in complete amazement. After an explosive, "That is so not true!" I began rattling off the many gifts and achievements David had accomplished: writing two books, creating many anointed worship songs and publishing them, playing the pipe organ, bass and accordion, not to mention his incredible piano playing and vocal skills and being an excellent Bible teacher! He was also hysterically funny and entertaining, so his statement made no sense to me.

David's belief that he was somehow less than me and others, had completely distorted his perception of reality. There was a massive lie blocking him from living out of his true identity. This in turn affected the way he related to me. Believing lies is something we all do, including me. Our lies can make us deaf and blind to the truth about who we are and what God has for us. If we don't allow God to work in our hearts and heal us, the truth stays on the outside of us and cannot affect change inside.

I had just begun my journey of seeing myself the way God does when I entered Christ for the Nations Bible School back in 1979. Sally Horton, who was a leader over the women there, encouraged me to acknowledge and "let in" other's affirmations. I had gone to see her to get help with some depression and struggles with insecurity. She began by counseling me to say, "thank you, I receive that" to every person who said anything positive or encouraging to me. She encouraged me that this was going to radically change my perspective on myself. It was really embarrassing at first, but over several weeks' time of choosing to receive compliments, I began to feel differently, and to hear differently. My views on myself were changing because I was letting truth in. How often do we resist positive words by deflecting the loving affirmation others are giving us? Let God transform the way you see yourself! Doing so is important not only for today, but also for your future and for your relationships and your destiny.

While I was waiting for a partner I struggled against the lie that there was something wrong with me if a man didn't come into my life. I must not be attractive enough, or good enough. Because of the depth of this lie, there were some years when I waited with grace, and other times when I didn't. I went through many years of feeling completely satisfied with being a single mom and woman. There were seasons when I felt lovely and attractive. There were months and years when I felt completely fulfilled with being single. Then I'd cycle back into the deep longing of wanting to share life with someone and to have someone to partner with share the load. Then the fear, the power of that lie, would rise up again --- fear that marriage might not happen, fear that I wasn't enough for someone or that I was too much for someone. Cycling thoughts would invade my mind once again. In the times when I waffled in my confidence in God, I would once again try internet dating, or give a reminder to friends that I was still alive and remind them to keep their eyes open for a potential mate for me. In those seasons I really struggled for my soul to be at rest concerning a future mate.

I had blind dates, and friend-referral dates but, all in all, I didn't date a lot during the waiting years. In total I had two more serious relationships of a few months in length. I went out with men just enough for me to keep discovering and defining things about myself with every date. I learned I couldn't be with someone I wasn't attracted to. I worked through feeling selfish about being so picky plus the awkwardness of saying no to some godly, kind men, but there was simply no point in dating when there was no attraction. I evaluated and defined what I needed and wanted in a husband, right down to things like where I wanted to live and where I didn't; whether I wanted younger children or not; and other equally practical and specific issues. I became comfortable with myself and with having opinions about the things I wanted and needed out of a relationship.

During the fourteen plus years of singleness, I settled the issue internally that I wasn't enough, and learned to rest in the reality that God was protecting me from the wrong kind of man. I'd asked Him to keep me safe from my own broken mechanisms and blindness and He had done just that. I made good use of books, underwent healing prayer, and did personal evaluations in order to keep a healthy attitude toward my singleness.

I've had numerous women ask me how I dealt with dating and staying pure in both body and heart over the years of being alone. I daily asked Jesus to keep me safe from my own weaknesses --- even the ones I wasn't aware of. I knew my vulnerabilities with the physical, having been married before, so I chose not to go to places where there was alcohol or dancing, places where I knew I'd be tempted. I didn't let my mind wander or go to fantasy which could have made me spiral mentally and emotionally. I made myself accountable to people I could trust, people who would ask me hard questions, anytime I embarked on a new relationship. Face to face accountability with prayer was what I looked for from these friends, and they were faithful to that invitation.

I also worked on being present for my kids and with the friends I had made. I reminded myself that I was part of the Body of Christ and that what I did affected those around me. I chose joy and thankfulness instead of focusing on what I didn't have. I stayed busy serving in ministry and work. I made a specific, detailed list of the attributes of character I wanted and needed in a husband. I prayed over this list, submitting it to the Lord, and determined in my heart not to settle for less. However, all these preventative measures were not enough to keep me completely safe, as I learned several years later.

In my seventh year of being single, I had several prophetic words through people that my partner was coming quickly. The words were all similar in language and not provoked by me in any way, so I became almost certain that God was bringing my husband that year. I foolishly and independently, without the Holy Spirit's guidance, decided to try going out with some men that weren't as sold out in their faith as I was. I set myself up for failure and shame with my independence. I was saying to myself, "I can handle this on my own." And guess what? Along came a man that didn't fit any of my list of what I wanted and needed, except for one huge piece: he "got" me. He wasn't intimidated by me. He affirmed me. He was really attracted to me, something my heart hadn't had assurance of in my first marriage. David had liked me dressed "to the nines" and looking finished and polished, but this guy liked me with no makeup on. He soothed lots of insecurities in my soul and I plunged into the relationship with both feet, ignoring every whisper of warning from the Holy Spirit. At the time, I didn't even recognize I was ignoring God, but a few short months later I did. However, by then I had fallen in love with the idea of this man and the way he enjoyed me as a person, and by the way he seemed to not need me.

Sadly, I compromised some of my physical boundaries, so we mutually decided to part ways, realizing we weren't the best for each other. I never spoke to him again. It was agonizing and shameful for me that I'd jeopardized my commitment to purity, agonizing because I had started to let my heart feel again, agonizing in the disappointment that the man God had for me still wasn't here. The inappropriate weight I'd given the prophetic words from others and my impatience over waiting for someone combined to block the promptings from the Lord Who was trying to protect me. As a result, I was hurting more than I should have been.

Because of my stance on purity and my teaching about this, the shame I felt over what I'd done, was almost unbearable. I knew there was only one way to deal with it and that was to confess my failure to my leaders at the time. I was determined to embrace what I challenged others to do. I wanted to break the power of shame over my life, quit hiding my sin, and receive my inheritance of forgiveness. I knew I had to act quickly and decisively. I was terrified and yet very hopeful that my leaders would be loving in their response, and they were. I told them to ask the hard questions, and they did. They very lovingly rebuked me and called me up higher.

Oh what freedom there is in confession! Confessing our sins opens the door to healing. I can't tell you how many people I've seen in the counseling room who are in their fifties and are confessing to me something that happened 30 years prior that they have never shared. Consequently, they have been bound by the event and the shame brought on by it ever since. The Bible says, "Confess your sins one to another that you may be healed."[45]

After our breakup and my confession, I began to grieve. For the next six weeks I grieved, grieved the loss of a possibility, the confusion over the encouraging prophetic words, the giving up of something I

---

[45]*The Holy Bible, New Living Translation*, James 5:16 .

wanted so desperately. I grieved over the longing to be loved and accepted and protected by a man. I wailed, and my ministry partner Rebecca prayed for me. One morning she shared with me that she had a visitation from the Father and some of it had to do with me. She shared that Jesus was saying to her how much He loved me and that there was no shame that He could see. I took this literally as a word for me and began a dialogue with the Lord about the past several months. Why hadn't He stopped me? He very lovingly, very directly said, "You were in rebellion, Laurie". I responded internally. "Nooooo. What do You mean Lord?" I honestly didn't think I had any rebellion in me! But He firmly stated it was there. He gently reminded me of each time He'd warned me about where I was headed, and each time I had adamantly said, "I can handle this! I'll be ok." I suddenly saw my independence and that it was rebellion. What a shock! As I repented and wept over my blindness and the kindness of a Savior who does not lose hope in us over our sin, I began to truly heal.

Several years later, I had another potential opportunity for failure in the relationship arena. I again was going through fresh longings to be married. Instead of saying no, I connected with a guy on Facebook that I'd gone to High School with. After having a dinner date with him and realizing he was not on the same page spiritually, I still agreed to talk with him on the phone. After the incident shared previously, I had always had tight accountability with close friends about who I was seeing or talking to, as an extra measure of safety. But, even though I had a housemate living with Brynne and me at the time, I failed to mention that I had had a few conversations with this man.

God is so kind! He lets us pull on the strings of His protection because He wants us to desire His protection and invite it. In the last phone conversation with this man, he asked if he could see me when he was visiting my city. I said I'd think about it. I got off the phone, questioning myself over the wisdom of connecting with him, and said to the Lord out loud, "If I'm not supposed to go out with this guy, please make it really clear!" I went to bed and the following morning there was an email from my housemate Ashley, sharing that she'd had a dream about me. In the dream I was talking to some guy without her knowing about it. She asked if this was true, and I was so shocked I reacted by swearing out loud, "Holy s… ! You are serious Lord!" I could not believe that He would so quickly and literally answer my prayer and lead me so kindly. I immediately wrote the guy and explained that we couldn't continue talking any more. The Lord will protect us if we let Him and obey.

When I got to church that next Sunday morning, the Holy Spirit was prompting me to testify of what had just happened. I was trying to convince myself that this was not God, when a friend and counselor approached me and said the Lord was giving me a clear exhortation to give the Body. So, in obedience, I went to my leaders and submitted that I had something to share on obedience. They did not often hand over the mic, but my pastor looked at me and said, "Go for it". I can't remember half of what I shared, but the Holy Spirit's focus was on waiting for God's Isaac, and not settling for Ishmael, trusting God to bring what we need, and obeying His directives which lets Him protect us. Even in my going down that path of hidden independence again, the Father was redeeming my foolishness and bringing encouragement, warning, and directives through it. It is so important that we follow Him.

I gave that word on a Sunday; little did I know that within a year I would finally meet the one my heart longed for. I know in my heart that the Father gave me a second chance, something He has done with me over and over, extending His mercy and offering another chance to learn obedience and dependence on Him.

In your waiting to find a spouse, many of you may have tried internet dating, while others may have been hesitant to engage the web for help in connecting. After my experiences with several sites over many years, my encouragement would be this: there is always the need for discernment and "vetting" by people you trust of anyone you meet, whether in person or online. I was scammed many times by fake people with fake profiles. Most of the time I listened to the Holy Spirit when I felt in my gut that something wasn't right, but occasionally I disregarded it and kept talking with someone that eventually proved to be not a healthy person. That pattern of disappointment can lead to hope deferred. One of my worst dates was set up by a friend, so it's not always safe to go that route either. Always listen to the Holy Spirit and to your trusted friends. Bring them into the entire process.

After so many years of waiting, and receiving prophetic words, I began lamenting over my unsuccessful dating relationships and wondering if I was a fool to continue to believe. Perhaps I was not even supposed to get married?

As previously stated, when we receive a prophetic word, we need to wait on God for the fulfillment. We need to exercise caution and weigh the prophecy carefully. I had assumed that the prophecy given to me about finding a new husband quickly meant it would happen in my earthly timetable's definition of quickly. We humans have a tendency to interpret the prophecies others present to us within the framework of our experience and from the context of our own needs. It is much safer to hold the prophetic with an open hand, discerning with the help of the Holy Spirit and with the input of others we trust, what is from God and what is not, and what it means for our lives. I've watched too many people make important decisions based on a word a prophet gave without carefully judging the word and waiting for confirmation. Such naiveté and inappropriate trust often results in disappointment, disillusionment, broken hearts and dreams. As I share in my next chapter, receiving prophecy with discernment, and holding it loosely, is vital.

I only had the Lord speak to me personally about marriage one time in the 14 plus years I was single. He said, "I'm bringing you a man of stature." It was helpful to hold onto that statement, but it was still difficult to weigh the other words that were given to me. The longer I waited, the more difficult it became. On a side note, our God has a sense of humor! I must share my take on what the Lord meant by a man of stature. From the time that He said this phrase to me, I felt He was smiling in a teasing way and that my husband to be was not going to be tall. I know that may sound crazy, but I would hear Him chuckle!

I shared this with my kids, and my son Collin quipped, "Mom, you know what kind of man that is. He means a man of influence". But my impression was that God was having fun with me and making a play on words. I was sure of this and it would make me smile. There is more to come on this, but I eventually found that God actually was teasing me! He was pushing back the way a father would and challenging my judgment that I needed a tall man.

In His kindness, the Father eventually brought me a word I could trust while waiting for my man of promise. A prophet I very much respect, who does not normally give words about marriage, happened to be hanging out at my daughter Heather's home in 2011. I jokingly informed him it was my birthday and asked if he had a word for me. I'll never forget the disgruntled look on his face when I said this, but a while later he said the Lord had something for me. He spoke a short but specific word about the season I was entering and what the Father had planned. I wrote it all down and hid it in my heart. The word started out by saying that the season I was in was ending, like rags being taken off and new clothes being given to me. The word didn't feel super significant until the man said, "and in this season you will be yoked and it will be the yoke of marriage". He then listed three specific things about the man I was to meet: he was a pioneer, he had a shepherd's heart, and he had a prophetic gift that he didn't quite understand. He also said that my guy's sphere of influence would help mine and vice versa. Needless to say, I was encouraged, and I held on to that word, declared that word, thanked God for that word, but I also let it rest in the Father's hands. Four and a half years later, I needed to seek input from others, weigh the word again, and hold the man I'd met up to the words that had been spoken.

In my experience working with relationships and marriages, there are always subconscious things that draw us to another person, things that come out of old family imprints, familiar things, and even unhealthy mindsets. In addition, the Father Himself draws us together. During the waiting process, I kept working on my wrong expectations, and I intentionally tried to identify any skewed beliefs I had about men

94

or relationships. I knew that there would be more things to come up after I was actually in a relationship, but I was determined to uncover and get healed of everything that could block a healthy man from being drawn to me, or that could cause a relationship to have more conflict than necessary. I wanted to be my most authentic, most healed, self going into a new relationship.

A few years into my process, I went to receive some healing work from a friend. While she was working with me, she quietly said, "You believe that men aren't safe". In my rational mind, I was taken aback, but my heart resonated with what she said. My past was distorting my present perceptions! The lie that "men aren't safe" had been buried in my subconscious for a long time, but I was completely unaware of it. I even remembered some friendships I had had with men and thought how much I enjoyed and liked men, but underneath my thoughts there was this belief, with loads of distrust attached to it. I began reviewing my history with men in my journey and looking at the ways I was treated that supported this mistrust.

Over the next few months I was deliberate in connecting with the Lord and renewing my mind and I broke agreement with this belief. I came to realize that the lie was planted when I was a young woman and received lots of negative male attention concerning my body. The lie was strengthened by the infidelities in my marriage and by male leaders who discounted me because of me being a woman. Most of us don't realize that our history has made a profound impact on our minds and perspectives, both for good and for bad. Despite my own history, as I worked intentionally on changing my distorted perceptions, I made the shift to walk in the truth. Today, when I'm speaking, I share that I truly believe that if I had not fully resolved this lie, it could have delayed or interrupted my meeting Tim, my future husband. At the very least, it could have produced numerous places of conflict between us because the lie is fear-based and would have created suspicion. It is important, while you are single, that you deliberately examine memories of times when you have been wounded so that you will not be set up for trouble in your future by unhealthy repeats of those patterns of pain.

Find yourself in Jesus and be fully who you are without a man! Pour out to others less strong than you. I volunteered for a ministry called The Single Mom KC for several years as a pastoral director and counselor, to be a voice of hope and encouragement to other women raising families alone. It kept me focused outward and not inward. Let the waiting (patience) have its full work --- it's worth it.[46]

Father God, would you meet my brother or sister in this place of waiting and loneliness? Would You visit them with Your comfort and grace and resolve as You did me? Holy Spirit, lead their steps in a straight path and give them what they need to live in a place of expectation and hope in regards to their dreams and longings. Surround them with others who will stand with them. Expose wrong mindsets that are keeping them stuck! Heal family imprints and break unhealthy patterns. Protect them from themselves and others who are not sincere. If they have compromised in their waiting, wash them anew and bring resolve to wait for Your best. Heal their hearts and give them grace and joy in the waiting.

Here I am, Lord, again
On my knees once again
Waiting for You
I see my sin once again
Need your cleansing again
Wash me anew

Amazing, amazing Your love
Poured out for me such love
Amazing, amazing Your grace
You suffered in my place

---

[46]Misty Honnold, president of The Single Mom KC, a ministry to single moms.

Overwhelming love always new each day
Overwhelming grace wipes my sin away!
Your blood shed for me, forgiveness eternal and free
Your blood shed for me, forgiveness eternal and free!

Amazing, amazing Your love
Poured out for me such love
Amazing, amazing Your grace
You suffered in my place

Here I am Lord again, on my knees once again...

Laurie Goddu ©

Chapter 7: Worth the Wait: My Man of Promise

As I shared previously, Brynne and I ended up living in a basement apartment with our friends Rustin and Laura in Grandview, Missouri. Through our four-plus year journey of living with them, they diligently were praying and watching for a man for me. They loved being matchmakers and Laura is an amazing connector, though nothing came of their attempts to set me up with a godly man.

One day in October 2014, several years into our time living there, Laura met me on the stairs to tell me that she had cleaned the home of a man who had just moved here and that he was a widower. She excitedly shared that she felt he'd be perfect for me. My interest was piqued! I asked a few typical questions like: "Is he attractive; is he a man of leadership and integrity;" and, with a smile, "Is he tall enough?" Laura answered, "Yes!" to all my questions. I told her that she should set us up for a coffee date. She gave me a thumbs up and I began praying for this man and his family who had suffered loss. I knew nothing of where he came from or what the situation had been, but I knew how to pray for others who were grieving, from my own losses. A few weeks later, I was upstairs and asked Laura what had happened with setting up the coffee date. She responded that her husband had said it was too soon for this man to engage in dating. I asked what he meant, and Laura told me that it had only been six months since his wife's passing. I sighed a deep sigh; I knew Rustin was right.

I continued to pray for the man and his family for several more days, but finally said out loud to the Father, "I'm done praying for this guy. If you want me to meet him, You are going to have to bring him to me!" I released that hope and did not think about him again. I had no idea how significant this exchange had been. From October 2014 until July 2015 the Father was working His divine preparations for me and orchestrating events that were strategic for my future.

There are too many details to share, but these are the highlights. For several months my dear friend Marion had been asking me to join her at a conference in Dallas. I kept saying no, and she kept telling me the Holy Spirit was telling her I needed to come. I finally agreed. This was in September. Then in October the Holy Spirit said to attend a Patricia King conference locally in Kansas City. This was more conferences in one month that I had attended in the previous five years. This was not my normal!

At the conference in Dallas, the Lord brought two very significant prophetic encouragements to me. One was about my music and doing another CD, and the other was about the restoration of all things in my life. To me, the most significant thing about the download the Holy Spirit brought was through a prophetic word given about restoration by Dutch Sheets to all the conference attendees. He wasn't even scheduled to speak that night. Having my old pastor and friend deliver a word about restoration was like the Lord highlighting the prophecy in neon lights! I felt like I was in a private funnel in the midst of thousands of people. I was weeping deeply and I felt faith igniting in me to agree with what the Lord was saying. Hope welled up and I knew the impartation was very significant.

There was also a confronting question presented by the Holy Spirit at the Patricia King conference I attended a month later. A corporate word came that deeply connected with me in which the Lord declared, "I want you for myself!" This word had a profound impact on me. I had been dialoguing with the Holy Spirit about the jealousy of Jesus for

His bride, and had been receiving new revelation about His jealous love for me. Though I was in the middle of a crowd and no one spoke directly to me, I still felt personally and intimately confronted by Jesus. This experience caused me once again to question whether I would be disappointing God or missing His best if I remarried. An internal war began inside of me. I wrestled with God for the next several months, trying to determine what He meant when He said, "I want You for myself." I finally was able to settle with certainty that I could have both a husband and a heart that was all the Lord's. I realized that if I remarried my heart still must be fully given and dependent on the Lord. Receiving a partner would not take away my need to depend upon Jesus. How true this realization has proven to be!

The last challenge mentally came in May 2015. I had been telling Rustin and Laura that I wanted to get out of the "holy hole" (my basement apartment). I like light and the basement was dark, and I felt closed in. At the same time, I was wrestling with the overwhelming thought of moving again, alone. I looked at houses and apartments but would waffle every time I was supposed to commit to a lease. There just wasn't peace in my heart. I finally found a place that was everything I'd been looking for and on the day I was to sign the lease, a God-ordained conversation took place with my pastor Adam that changed everything.

After our corporate gathering that Sunday, Adam, and I randomly began talking about the spiritual season we were in. I shared that I'd been hearing the Lord say for months, "What's in your heart, Laurie?". In response, I'd been saying, "Whatever You want, Lord". As I shared this with Adam, he became excited and shared that he had been having the same conversation with the Lord, but His conversation was pertaining to our church moving locations. We were each asking God if He wanted us to move when the Father was actually asking us to tell Him what we wanted! God wanted to give us our desires and was inviting us to declare our hearts to Him. In that moment the wrestling stopped and I made a decision not to move out of the basement and not to sign the lease on the new house. I began declaring to the Lord,

"I won't move, Lord, until You bring me my husband to do it with me." God wanted me to tell Him what I wanted, so I did!

There was a major shift in my expectation of God's provision when I agreed with my own heart's desire. Faith is activated when the fear that has been driving us is exposed and released. The lie may have been buried but its exposure gives us a new capacity to choose to reject it and believe the truth. When we receive new insight and truth, new expectations are birthed in us, which leads to hope, and hope is very powerful. Romans 15:13 says that we will be filled with all hope and joy in believing through the power of the Holy Spirit.[47] The Father had been talking to me about the power of my expectations (my hopes), both positively and negatively, for the past several years. He patiently kept bringing it around to me until I got it.

As June came around, a friend of mine who volunteered for Single Mom KC came to my home to teach a dating seminar. After his sharing time, I approached him to ask if he could give me any suggestions for meeting some mature Christian men. His response irritated me when he suggested internet dating. I let him know I'd already "been there and done that" with no success. I had basically made a vow several years before that it would take at least three dreams and a vision for me to try internet dating again. Rick said a couple of times over the evening, "You should pray about it." I finally came to the conclusion a week later that I should probably break agreement with the vow I'd made and at least ask the Lord about trying internet dating again. It was a bit surprising when I heard nothing from the Lord, neither a yes nor a no.

As I continued waiting and listening, and not sensing a no, I began casually looking at sites online and seeing if any drew me. There was still no specific direction from the Father. I began filling out a new profile with a new moniker, (a site name) just in case I heard something from the Father. Then, in July, I did feel a drawing to a dating website called Christian Mingle. It was smaller than most sites, and it had been

---

[47] *Amplified Holy Bible*, Romans 15:13.

the first site I'd tried many years before. The latter part of July, I began checking profiles for widowers several times a week. I still had not signed up for the site, but I didn't want to sign up unless there were some men who appeared to meet my standards.

One night, just before I was to fly out to Colorado Springs, I saw on the Christian Mingle Site an icon with a star that said, "favorites". I clicked on the icon, not knowing what it stood for, and a profile of a widower came up. He was attractive, and his profile was simple and straightforward. Christian Mingle said we were a 93% match, yet he had not shown up on any of my searches for the area I lived in. I was excited that he had reached out, and I promptly sent him a smiling emoji. An emoji was the only response I was allowed as a non-paying member. Within hours there was mail in my box indicating someone had contacted me. I panicked and called my dear friend Libby to have her help me figure out what to do. Should I join so I could read the note? What if it was negative? What if he was notifying me he was in a relationship? Libby lovingly lit into me. "Pay the fee so you can read the note! We have been praying for years for a mate for you!"

I sheepishly joined the site. After reading the note I was a bit disappointed when it was only one line, albeit a positive one line. Throughout the following week while I was in the Springs, the gentleman and I conversed through email and eventually by phone. By late in the week, he asked if we could meet in person sooner rather than later, just to get a feel for whether we would like to continue talking. It was easy to say yes, since there had been several things he'd shared about his history that made me feel that he was a safe person and solid in his character. He was also reading one of my favorite marriage books on communication, *How We Love* by Milan Yerkovich, which was encouraging to me. The family I was staying with in the Springs was also excited to track with me and my conversations with this new acquaintance whose name was Tim.

The following Monday evening after returning home, as I was coming up the basement stairs dressed for my first date with Tim, my landlord Laura saw me and commented on how cute I looked and asked where I was going. I sheepishly told her I had a date. She was really surprised and asked how I had a date and she didn't know about it. I quickly explained that I had joined a dating website and been conversing with the guy while I'd been out of town. As any good friend would, she then demanded I show her his picture. I hesitated, because I knew the guy was on his way to the house, but she insisted I pull up his Facebook page. I did so and she looked at my phone, then me, then the phone, and exclaimed, "It's him!". I replied, "Him who?" and she replied, "The guy from October. The one whose house I cleaned!" I responded, "That's impossible!" Laura insisted that Tim was the same guy she had wanted me to meet almost a year before who lived on Indiana Ave. I was stunned! My thoughts began racing and I sent up a one second prayer asking the Lord to help me to set aside the thought that He just might have brought Tim to me in fulfillment of His promise. I needed to be composed and calm for this first date. Then my phone dinged and I had to go out and meet him.

The poor guy knew nothing of my interchange with Laura or my history of praying for him. After shaking hands and climbing into his car, he asked if I was ok. I was trying diligently to think of the appropriate thing to say and settled with "I think you might know my landlord." And then proceeded to share she had cleaned his house the day he moved to Kansas City. He acknowledged he remembered her and we moved on from that first awkward moment for me. Later he told me I looked like a deer in the headlights!

Our first date was great so we kept talking. I even texted my pastor after our first date, suggesting that he meet Tim. Tim had led urban missional communities the bulk of his life and our church was formed around missional communities. I knew Tim would be a great connection for Adam, even if we didn't keep on seeing each other.

The next few weeks of seeing Tim and getting to know him were a whirlwind. Again and again, I had to lay at the Lord's feet my past prophetic words. It quickly became apparent that he was a solid, mature, steady man of God. He had been married to his late wife Janet for almost 38 years. They had done full-time ministry together in the urban core for most of their married life on both the east and west coasts. He had served as a missionary and in the top tier of leadership with World Impact. To top it off, he had a sense of humor and enjoyed playfully teasing me. We each called on trusted friends to hold us accountable and to use their discernment in "checking out" each other as we proceeded to get to know one another. One of his friends asked me why I was attracted to Tim and I told her it was because he's a man of prayer --- and that he had beautiful blue eyes!

Many women have asked me since then how I set aside the prophetic words and only focused on what I was seeing and experiencing with Tim. I had seen so many people deeply hurt by "following a word," and not honestly evaluating real situations or relationships or receiving input from others. I was adamant that by God's grace I wasn't going to do that. In addition, I had experienced what seemed to be a supernatural connection with my first husband David when we were dating. I did not ask questions or evaluate the relationship beyond what I thought I had heard from the Lord and what I felt emotionally. God had told me my husband would be unfaithful, but I assumed the unfaithfulness would only happen once and that I was "made" for overcoming this kind of situation. How wrong I was! I was not going to make that mistake again.

Along the way, as we got to know one another better and better, we had some confirmations from other people, including one of Tim's daughters, who had a dream about her dad starting to see someone. In the final analysis though, it was mostly our interactions and conversations with one another that led us to keep dating. We took personality tests and assessments on gifts to help bring clarity and assurance as well. I vetted him with many of my friends and he did the same with me.

I not only had the old prophetic words to daily leave with Jesus, but a very supernatural event happened about three weeks into our dating. Only a handful of my closest friends knew I was going out with Tim, and a client I'd seen in the past called me out of the blue saying he had an important prophetic word for me, and he wanted to see me as soon as possible. I told him I was open to hearing the word, but asked that my friend and roommate Ashley be present for it. I just had an impression that someone was supposed to be there to witness his word. I also felt we were to record it.

The night arrived and my client began sharing what the Lord had shown him. I was resonating overall with what he was sharing about my ministry and some shifts coming in my future. Then he described seeing two defibrillators vibrating and then coming together. He declared that God was bringing the two defibrillators together and that this represented a marriage. I was floored and he was quite surprised as well. He turned to me and said, "It's almost like you have already met him." I didn't say a word. I was too dumbfounded! The next thing he said and did, astounded me even more. He turned toward my dining room wall and declared, "This is weird, but the Lord says to tell you, He's tall enough." As he spoke those words, he put his hand on the wall marking about 5'8"-9". I began sobbing and we had to hit pause for a minute. Unbeknownst to both Ashley and my client, I had given Tim a birthday card the weekend before. On the inside of the card I'd written an acronym of his name. After each letter I wrote a short statement about his character. On the second T, I had written "tall enough". The Holy Spirit had instructed me to do this and here God was confirming through someone else that I was supposed to marry this specific man!

Remember my sharing about the private joke with God, "I'm bringing you a man of stature"? Well, Tim was 5'9" and just tall enough, in my estimation, and obviously in the Father's as well. God certainly does have a sense of humor. The word went on to describe our getting married and that our ministry together was going to involve putting things in order apostolically in the Church and possibly even in business. Many other confirming things were declared that night, including that this man was a man of influence. I was so glad we had recorded what was shared prophetically, because it was definitely a sign and a wonder.

I wept with gratefulness, yet simultaneously felt fear at what had occurred. How was I going to keep this out of the mix when moving forward with a relationship with Tim? How was I going to avoid letting it direct me while still allowing it to be the confirmation I needed? And why was God giving me all this information and confirmation?

I immediately contacted several other close friends to bring them into the loop with keeping me accountable emotionally. In the past, I had asked the Lord many times to make it clear when He brought me someone, but this felt ridiculous! It reminded me of the word the Lord had spoken to me in the past, "I love you over the top ridiculous!"

After several weeks of dating, long walks, and talking a lot, I asked Tim one night how he felt about our time together. He thought a few seconds, then replied, "It's a green light until it's a red light!" I laughed and said, "That's great that it's a green light, but that is not a feeling word. May I suggest some words and you pick the one that fits?". This interchange was the first of many indicators that Tim was nothing like my late husband, and I loved that. Even though he was not a deep emotional communicator at that point, he was so willing to learn. Our relationship moved forward steadily and quickly and by Thanksgiving we were talking of a future together. At this point I asked Tim if he was ready to hear of the prophetic things the Father had spoken to me through the years. He said he was ready so I shared with him the prophetic words I had received concerning a future husband. He was blown away but greatly encouraged. He had had nothing like that kind of direction from the Lord in his journey, and God had not spoken to him about me. What an amazing Father we serve, how kind He is and how consistent in leading us wisely.

As we moved forward and considered Tim and Janet's kids and how challenging our marriage could be for them (Janet had passed less than two years before), we asked the Father for wisdom and favor in how to love them well. I committed to them that I wouldn't push my relationships with them. We both held to the conviction that "love doesn't demand its own way". Interestingly, in Tim's oldest daughter's dream she'd heard from the Lord, the words "safe and sweet", as she saw her dad and a woman in the dream, at an event. This dream helped prepare her for our relationship. "Safe and sweet" were the words we used to describe our dating relationship and eventual wedding ten months later.

Friends were concerned that it would be a big transition for me, having been single for so long. I expected that it was not going to be hard, and I was correct. God had done a thorough work of preparation and healing in my heart and mind. All the intentional work I did on my heart to bring healing from my painful history was complete. I had shifted in my evaluation of what was important in a relationship. I say regularly that getting married and living with Tim has been the easiest transition of my life. I believe this is because I did the hard work of change and looking at hard stuff while I was still single!

We reminded ourselves throughout our dating that the reward was worth the wait. I say emphatically, Tim is so worth the wait! A steadfast, faithful man who is strong in his identity; a protector and a man who knows and lives the Word of God; a man whose gifts and personality compliment mine for God's Kingdom purposes --- yes, he is worth the wait! I'd always said to the Lord, "Give me a marriage where we are better together than we are apart." God did exactly that.

Father, would you help each person waiting for Your best to wait patiently?

Comfort and strengthen them in their identity. Expose old wounds that could make them vulnerable to missing what and who is Your provision for them.

Bring them a partner who will enhance who they are and balance them as you have me. Awaken both their hearts to one another wherever they are.

I wrote this song during my waiting for Tim. It was written to Jesus, my Husband for those fourteen years. Press into the One Who loves you best and the most. He gave everything for us!

Awaken my heart to Your Love
Awaken my heart to Your love
It's better than wine, it's better than bread
It's better than the love of men, You are!

I wait, I hope, expecting Your love
I wait, I hope, expecting Your love

Drinking from Your cup my heart is satisfied
Eating from Your Word is more than enough
You are the living waters restoring my soul
You are the Bread of life, my all in all

Leaning into You my heart is at rest
My hope my glory, left peace and breath
You are the Living waters restoring my soul
You are the breath of life my all in all

Laurie Goddu ©

Chapter 8: More Stories and Encouragement

As I was walking one day and reviewing some of the amazing experiences and supernatural events that have happened to me, I realized that this could really be intimidating to someone who isn't sure God has ever spoken to them or given them prophetic leading. I don't want that to be the case. Each of our stories is unique and different. This is just my story. My life is supposed to be a prophetic picture of redemption and healing because that is who the Father made me to be. Along with the color and dramatic prophetic things that have happened in my journey are also lots of traumatic events. It is what it is. Please don't compare your story to mine unless it's to bring you hope and grace and strength!

Our God is a Redeemer, so in the economy of the Kingdom, I honestly don't believe there are mistakes. As I've already said, God always redeems and works something beautiful out of the hard and broken places. I invite you to trust Him with the shattered places of your life. He's creating a mosaic. Here are a few more pieces from mine.

Remember: God is with you and for you and He is leading you even when you are unaware. Ask Him to bring His divine connections.

When I was 11 years old, my entire family travelled to Europe for a six-week visit to meet my dad's family and friends, as he was from England. At the beginning of the trip we had a layover in Iceland. We were on a bus being transported in the night to another terminal when I had a profound experience of God's divine connections. My mom was chatting with a man sitting across from us. He had a heavy accent and dark skin and we soon learned he was from South America. As he and my mom continued to talk, she suddenly became very animated and exclaimed, "He knows Felipe!" I could not believe it! This random man sitting across from us on a bus in Iceland, was from Peru, and knew a man we had adopted as a foreign student studying in Midland, Michigan. Felipe was adopted family, present at our holiday gatherings. Meeting someone who knew him across the world, in the middle of the night ...What are the odds?

I distinctly remember pondering this information within the grid of our world and God. I knew from that moment on that God has divine connections for us in our journeys. Ever since that day I have asked for and expected that everywhere I go, God has a divine connection for me for His purposes. Those connections consistently happen. Why not ask Him for those connections yourself? Sometimes God's purpose turns out to be something simple like making a new friend, but other times those connections turn out to be a bridge to a bigger purpose God has for you. You may have a deposit to make in someone's life, or vice versa, something that will change the course of your life or theirs.

I'll share this divine connection story because it was so very special. On my return trip from ministering in South Africa with friends years ago, I had a prophetic evangelism encounter with a gentleman on my plane ride from London to the United States. We had been chatting through our meal and when we closed our eyes to go to sleep the Holy Spirit began telling me a list of things about the man. I decided that if it was really God speaking, it would all be there when I woke up. The words were still imprinted on my mind and heart after waking.

I tentatively asked this gentleman if I could share some things that God had shown me about him. I clarified that I was not a psychic but the insights I had were from God who loved him. He responded with, "certainly", and I began sharing: The Lord showed me that he was a gentleman, and also that he was a "gentle man", that those around him saw him as a tough guy, but he was really a softie at heart. God said that he had saved his life on at least three occasions, supernaturally preserving his life. The Lord said to me that he had worked for the cause of justice from the age of 10 or 11, and that this cause was very important to him. I shared that the Lord told me he was deeply dissatisfied with his life and God wanted to reveal Himself to him so that the second half of his life would be better than the first.

I finished sharing and the guy just kind of sat there. I told him I wouldn't bother him if he didn't want to talk, but he indicated he really wanted to respond. He said he was overwhelmed and was processing all I'd shared. Then he began to share some of his story. He confirmed all the facts the Lord had shown me with specific instances and stories. He shared how at five years old, as he and his mom drove up to the grocery in a Welsh village, God saved him by their car stopping an inch from a land mine. After he shared a couple more stories, I noticed he had still not addressed the injustice part of the word. I asked if he minded sharing what he did for a living. He smiled and hesitated, then said he was a cop. I responded with a smile, acknowledging the injustice piece in him. Then he leaned over and said, "There's more". He then stated that he worked for Scotland Yard in the Anti-terrorist Unit. I was floored! How cool is that? God knows just how much information to tell us. If I had known what he did for a living I would never have given my testimony so boldly to him, and certainly would have been more hesitant about sharing what God had shown me. Our Father knows just what to tell us, and what not to.

I prayed for this man for many months that the reality of God's love that was demonstrated through the words of knowledge God had given me would draw this man into a personal relationship with the living God. I won't know until heaven if he came to the Lord, but I know I did what God required of me on that plane.

God hears our secret petitions and is intricately involved in the details of our journeys.

When I was 13-16 years old I attended a Methodist church in Carmel, Indiana. An associate pastor named Reverend Miller worked with the youth group. He was so kind and so full of joy that he always stood out to me. When I received the Baptism of the Holy Spirit at the age of seventeen, I remember several times that year wondering if Reverend Miller might have been spirit-filled when I knew him in Carmel. He just radiated something different than the other leaders. Throughout my life I would say to the Lord that I'd love to know if my "hunch" was true. I have no idea why it stuck with me, or why it felt important, but God honored my request!

In the late 90's David and I were at a very large church in Colorado Springs doing a book signing. I was sitting in the church foyer greeting folks and chatting as David was autographing his book for people. As an older couple approached, I thought the man looked vaguely familiar. I asked him a few general questions and he shared that he had been a pastor. Several questions later it became clear that this was my former youth pastor from Indiana, Reverend Miller. I shared who I was and asked if he remembered me. He nodded affirmatively and gave me a hug. I gingerly asked if by any chance he had been spirit-filled way back when he was a youth pastor. He said yes! I began weeping with wonder at the kindness of the Lord to fill me in on this small but important detail in my life. Over 20 years had gone by since I'd seen Reverend Miller, but God had planted him securely in my memory and validated my young-woman impressions of him.

Tim, while leading missional communities for the ministry, World Impact, had never owned a home with his late wife Janet. He expressed a desire to own a home, so we began praying the first year of our marriage for the right place for us. We had a specific list of things we desired in our home and prayed about it regularly. We wanted a remodeled home with a separate entrance for an office, room for kids to visit, green space behind us, an open floor plan that was updated, and we needed the house to be in our price range. We planned to look seriously for a home in 2018, but we began casually looking at potential houses much earlier.

One Monday, which happened to be a vacation day for both of us, we were walking and praying when I commented that because the real estate market was crazy in Kansas City, we needed God to help us find a house before it hit the market. We prayed right then and asked the Lord to do that very thing. Later that same day, I saw an alert for a Facebook tag, something I'm not real familiar with. I opened it and both Tim's and my names were tagged to call a guy in our fellowship, because there was a house next door to him that was going on the market that evening. Our friend didn't know what we wanted in a home, but thought we should check it out. We called the realtor and he showed it to us at 5pm, just before it was being posted on the internet. We walked into the home and couldn't believe our eyes as one thing after another on our wish list was being checked off. We immediately asked what it would take to get the house, and the realtor said $1000 earnest money. I looked at Tim and he looked at me, both of us internally shaking our heads.

I had felt impressed to put my checkbook in my purse as that very day I had received a tax refund of just over $1000, exactly the amount we needed to hold the house! The gentle whisper of the Holy Spirit had made our path straight. The house was everything we wanted and needed and the time frame for moving fit our schedules exactly.

During the next six weeks, as we packed up and prepared to move, both of us alternately experienced a touch of buyer's remorse, mainly because the purchase decision had moved so quickly. Tim likes to do research as a part of his processing so our quick decision was a big step of faith for him. In addition, neither of us had a specific word from God to buy this house, but all the doors so flew open to purchase it that we did not think it was just a coincidence. We did a lot of praying as we packed, and God kept bringing peace.

As the closing day approached, it was delayed until July 7, 2017. Going to the mortgage lender's office that day to put down our final signatures, I was reminded of the date. We were signing the papers to buy our house on 07.07.17. God's number meaning perfection is seven, and there were three sevens in our closing date! Peace flooded me, knowing the Lord was highlighting once again His provision for this dream. Multiple sevens in the day's date were His sign to us that the house really was His gift and His desire for us.

Later it became obvious as we stepped into a more pastoral and coaching role with our fellowship, that this was exactly the house the Father wanted for us. Tim and I serve and help oversee a portion of our church body that is spread over a large geographic area. We did not know we would be involved in this ministry position when we bought the house, but God gave us the perfect house in the perfect location to fulfill this call on our lives. In addition, Tim resigned from Joni and Friends Ministry in January of 2018, a full year before we had thought he would. We now get to bless our own family and others with hosting, and our house has a comfortable office downstairs where I see clients. We asked specifically and God answered specifically. Our dream house came sooner than we expected because God knew that we would need it sooner than we expected.

The Spirit realm is real! Always remember this. Angels exist and so do demons.

I'll never forget a wild experience I had years ago while living in North Carolina. A new client came to see me and she began to tell me about her mom. Her mother worked with the police department there to help uncover satanic ritual locations and to investigate criminal activities of cults in the area. I felt a little nudge from the Holy Spirit that I needed to meet this client's mom as I had worked with some people in the past with backgrounds in satanic ritual abuse. I followed through and had the most astounding experience.

As I met with this woman in her home, she shared with me about a young man she'd led to Christ from a local satanic group. She pulled out a book of drawings that he had made of his "spirit guides" and of visions he had seen while serving Satan. The drawings were intricate and artistically perfect but very hideous and scary looking. As I was flipping through the artwork, the woman told me that this young man had recently disappeared from the nearby army base. She suspected that he had been killed by the satanic group he had been a part of because he had accepted Christ.

As I got to one of the last pages of his artwork, I almost jumped out of my skin because there was a drawing of a demon spirit that was almost a replica of a statue in a friend's home. My reaction was intensified because the week before, I'd had to go out to their home in the early morning hours because the smoke alarm kept randomly going off and her husband was out of town.

The troublesome alarm was outside the door of a room that had a number of artifacts and statues from overseas. One of the statues looked very much like the drawing I was looking at. The woman gave me permission to take the drawings to show the couple. I suggested they burn that specific wooden statue and they agreed it was a good idea. The little statue burned for several hours, even though it was a little 10-inch wooden statue.

For clarity's sake: People sometimes obtain artifacts and gifts from other cultures and countries that seem innocent or even beautiful but actually are spiritually polluted. I believe that these artifacts can often be prayed over and cleansed, spiritually. However, if they have been crafted for the purpose of idol worship, cleansing them may not be possible. My experience was a reminder that praying over foreign objects doesn't always work to cleanse them. There is a demonic realm that is very real.[48] We do not always understand how the unseen

---

[48] *Amplified Holy Bible,* Ephesians 6:12.

demonic realm can have an impact on us or how demons can attach themselves to inanimate objects, but idol worship is very real in some other countries. If we unknowingly bring an idol into our home, it can have surprising consequences. We must be discerning.

Although I do not like to glorify the demonic realm I had another experience in Sri Lanka that highlights the reality of the unseen forces of darkness. I was ministering at the home of my friends Woody and Melanie Blok. Their house was next door to people who did a lot of chanting through the night as they worshipped demonic "gods." One of the first nights I was there, I was awakened by a threatening presence in my room and I saw red eyes looking at me in the air next to my bed. I began to pray in tongues and spoke Bible verses out loud and the eyes eventually disappeared. The next morning I told my friends and they said they were familiar with this kind of demonic spirit and referred to it as a "watcher spirit." For the rest of my time there, I found that I needed to wear headphones and play worship music in order to sleep. The combination of unfamiliar idol worship and being in a foreign country made me more vulnerable to the spiritual atmosphere in Sri Lanka.

I'll finish with an angel story. When my husband Tim and I were volunteering with Joni and Friends at a Wheels for the World event in Guadalajara, Mexico, a few years back, we met a family who had gone through extreme tragedy. The family had been driving through Mexico, to go back to their home just across the border in the US. A few hours before they reached the border, their car was ambushed by supposed drug lords who had placed spikes on the highway to pop their tires. As the car careened out of control, it rolled and the husband was killed. The mom and one of her sons were seriously injured, the son so severely that he was paralyzed. As they lay beside the road in shock, trying to figure out what had happened, she shared that two people showed up at the wreck site to sit with her and the injured children until help came. As soon as the police arrived, the people who had been there disappeared. She was convinced that they were angels as the police never saw them or spoke with them. They were taken to hospitals and, after months of recovery, were now healing as a family. They were so thankful for God's provision that night for them, as well as for their receiving a new wheelchair for the son. The Bible tells us that God gives HIs angels charge over us, and that we have entertained angels unaware.[49]

He will equip you for what He's called you to.

Some of you who read my first book are aware of the Father's provision for His purposes in my daughter Brynne's life. She has a PDD diagnosis and so is on the spectrum for autism. She has succeeded beyond every negative limit that doctors gave, and all along the way, God gave us the coolest encouragement. I was working for a company called Brain Balance. This company performs assessments and evaluations on children with disorders of the brain and helps with brain integration for improvement with their weaknesses, i.e. ADD, ADHD, autism, Aspergers, language processing etc.

During the time I worked for Brain Balance, Brynne and I decided to have her assessed through their program. I'll never forget the director's response to us when we came in to hear the results of Brynne's assessment. With emotion in her voice, she shared that, according to Brynne's tests, she should not be able to --- or even want to --- work in an orphanage. But working in an orphanage was Brynne's dream. The director said that Brynne's desire and capacity for this dream were a testimony to the power of prayer and the strength of the Holy Spirit in her. The Holy Spirit was providing help and direction that Brynne did not have capacity for, based on the assessment's findings. Where Brynne was weak, Jesus was being strong. At the time of this writing, Brynne is 25 years old and has now lived and served in an orphanage in Sri Lanka for a total of a year, of the past 3 years,

---

[49]*Amplified Holy Bible*, Hebrews 13:2b "...[. . . sharing the comforts of your home and doing your part generously], for by this some have entertained angels without knowing it."

traveling there and back by herself! I was nervous, but the Lord was with her. She has expected God to fulfill her heart to serve, so when opportunities have come, she has gone. She lives in faith and hope, and loves others from that posture.

As I work with individuals and couples full time to help them heal from their past wounds, what an incredible joy it's been to watch the Lord transform lives. It's sometimes heavy stuff to hear and process, but the breakthroughs and transformations make the work so worth it! I've continually grown in my understanding of the body and the effects of trauma on it. God has blessed me with favor and with being networked with professionals and non-professionals who work with trauma and healing. I have ongoing relationships with other therapists and psychologists in the counseling field who are believers. We have referred clients to each other. I have taught both lay persons and professionals how to recognize severe dissociation from my personal experience of living with someone using this coping mechanism. None of these doors would have been open to me if I had not obeyed God's call to take a step and say yes. These opportunities did not arise because I was special; they came because I was obedient in the little steps He gave me that culminated in these invitations. God has always provided resources and individuals to teach me and to deepen my understanding of the things He wanted me to do. He will do the same for you. Don't be insecure in this! I wasted so many years feeling less-than because I didn't have a degree.

Even without that degree, God allowed me the privilege of working with a ministry in Houston, Elijah Rising, that works with victims of human trafficking. For a couple of years, I was able to teach and impart on understanding dissociation, since anyone who has been trafficked has utilized this mechanism at some level. Using Splankna was such an effective tool with these traumatized women. They were often unable to revisit their pain without it causing more trauma, so Splankna provided an alternative to healing other than traditional talk therapy. What a joy to play a part in their freedom and coming into the truth that the Father loves them and is for them! Helping them heal gave them the capacity to leave the past behind and move forward in their lives. God has prepared me and equipped me over many years with all that I needed to impart at the right moment to this ministry.

Renew your mind with His sanctified Word. Your brain has plasticity so there's hope for change.

Let the seeds of truth in God's Word be planted, watered, and nurtured in you as in the parable of the sower. In this parable there are all kinds of things that interfere with the seed taking root, but the seed that put down roots deep in the soil produced a crop. Remember, at the end of the story there is a reaping that comes in different proportions.[50] A healthy thought-life and the fruit of freedom from old hurts can be yours, but you must plant truth to reap it. Come into agreement with the truth of who God says you are and live out of your God-given uniqueness! Dr. Caroline Leaf is an expert on the brain and she shares that it takes 63 days for the green trees of the mind to become established as a new "forest" of belief so that it cannot be stolen.[51] Renewing your mind is a daily process. Transformation is a process. Come into agreement with what God says about you, who you are in your journey and in His heart. [52]

Be who you are! Don't try to emulate someone else other than Jesus. Who you are is completely special and the Father wants to move through your expression of His glory.

When I was younger I tried to be like the people I traveled with in ministry. I wanted to be like them in the way they operated in the gifts of the Holy Spirit we had in common. I was uncomfortable with who I

---

[50] Matthew 13:1-23, Mark 4:1-20, Luke 8:4-15.
[51] Dr. Caroline Leaf, speaking at The Rock of Kansas City, October 2017.
[52] Romans 12:1-2

was and I blocked the Holy Spirit from moving uniquely through me as He desired. I wanted to be like Cindy Jacobs and move in authority. I wanted to be able to sing and play like David did. That never happened, because I wasn't David, I was Laurie. I actually remember thinking when I was younger that I was a fraud and a fake, because I couldn't be like others I wanted to emulate. Just be you, even if that feels unoriginal!

Out of my intimate worship with Jesus, I've continued to write music. I've grown in my ability to play by ear on the keys and to flow prophetically. I didn't start learning to play by ear until David's passing, in my early 40's. There has also been fruit in worshipping for an audience of One. I feel the Father's pleasure when I play and sing for Him, and that's what matters most. Whether it's supporting worship teams or playing over single moms or clients, I'm myself, and who I am brings life to others.

It's not too late to start your dream or step out and express your gifts. Just be yourself. There is no one like you, never has been and never will be. Your way of demonstrating God's love, or gift, may be designed to touch a specific person no one else can reach.

Trust in the Father leading and guiding you. Worry does not bring life. Trust does. Grace is available today not in the past or future!

I heard a teaching years ago in which a Greek phrase in the New Testament was broken down to describe Jesus backing us into our future, like a person in a row boat with Jesus at the helm. I don't remember the exact Bible reference, but the imagery has stuck with me ever since. Many years later I had a dream related to this teaching. In my dream I was dancing with Jesus and I kept trying to look over His shoulder to see where we were going. He firmly but gently told me to look Him in the eyes. He said that He was backing me into my future.

This dream was brought back to life in my own personal journey recently. I had been confronting some old fears of disappointing authorities in my life and fighting to gain victory in my mind. The Holy Spirit told me to go and confess what I was feeling and ask for prayer from one of our elders. He and his wife listened to me and prayed for me. After they had declared love and truth to me, the gentleman took me in his arms and began to dance with me while Tim and his wife looked on. Tears streamed down my face as I remembered the dream from years before. Jesus had backed me into my future and it was all He had said it would be. He led me there and He had restored what appeared lost. God had promised me that the latter days would be greater than the former, and so they are. Pray out of Proverbs, "Cause my thoughts to become agreeable to Your will, Father,"[53] and lead my steps even when I plan my own way. He does and He will!

Use your authority in Christ to pray for others in your family for freedom and life.

You are a vanguard in your family. Some of us are pioneers and first-generation warriors, the first in our families called out of darkness into light. When I was in Bible school I had a dear friend who was also a powerful woman of prayer. Her name was Fiona, and she taught me much about the power of intercession. I was complaining one day about David not being a confidant leader in our home, and Fiona gave me a word of wisdom I've both appropriated in my own life and shared with many since. She taught that in marriage spouses have more power to pray for each other than anyone else because we are one. She instructed me to ask the Holy Spirit for Bible verses that spoke into areas in David's and my life that were not flourishing. I did this, picturing a tree with roots going down deeper and deeper as I spoke the verse God gave me from Job 14, "...that at the scent of water the tree will flourish and bring forth sprigs and shoots like a seedling."[54]

---

[53] *Amplified Holy Bible*, Proverbs 16:3 .
[54] *Amplified Holy Bible*, Job 14:9.

What a wonderful surprise when, a few months after praying, some of the things I'd prayed were being answered.

Because you and your spouse are one in the eyes of God, you have authority to pray for them like no one else. God also gives you authority to pray for your children with power and for your family. Step into that place in Christ and call things that are not as though they were in prayer over your loved ones. I've shared this with countless others and when they have applied this to their marriages, they have seen fruit! This principle was also demonstrated beautifully in the motion picture War room, when the main character discipled another woman to find scriptures to pray over her husband instead of complaining.[55]

God is always teaching us if we let Him. When you don't understand, keep asking questions.

Sometimes when we hear the Holy Spirit speaking, we know what to do and when to do it, but at other times it's not clear. Sometimes He brings something to our attention just so we will pray and petition the Father on someone's behalf. At other times God makes us aware of some truth so we can posture ourselves differently in prayer. At still other times, God is provoking us to action to do something.

For example, when I first moved to Kansas City in 2011, during my sabbatical, the Father kept highlighting the word deception. After several weeks of praying, I felt Him say that a shift had taken place in the earth and the full weight of the spirit of deception had been released. He wasn't telling me this so I could do something, instead He was calling me to watch and pray and be alert. Since that time, the acceleration in the earth of deception about many things --- about life in the womb, about gender issues, about what equality means --- has gone into a new level of craziness. I've been a watchman on the wall,

---

[55] Alex Kendrick, Director and Stephen Kendrick, Producer, *War Room*, Motion Picture (Culver City, CA: Affirm Films, Aug. 28, 2015).

praying that the elect would not be deceived, calling some away from the edge of a precipice of deception by pointing them to the Scriptures and what God says rather than relying on what they feel or what the culture says. God has anointed me to pray, but He has not told me to take any other action.

When I first moved to Fayetteville, NC, I remember stopping at a traffic light and the Father saying to me that one of the reasons He had moved us there was to teach me more about dissociation. I didn't know what that meant so I started asking more questions. Over the next few years, through clients and other relationships with people in the military, including doctors, I learned that the ability to dissociate is needed at a heightened level in those applying to be in special forces. This reality makes sense to me now with what I have learned about the mind and the body, but back then it didn't. When you don't understand what God is saying, keep asking questions.

I have also had the Holy Spirit highlight names on street signs and on passing truck ads to prompt me to pray for individuals by the same name. Many times I have received confirmation later, that those promptings were the Lord's, as the folks I prayed for were in need. All I did was ask, "Lord, how should I pray?"

One of the most profound life lessons I learned from God was related to the ways I operated in the gifts of the Holy Spirit. In my 30's, while traveling the world, I was exposed to a myriad of prophetic leaders in the Body of Christ. The Father kept highlighting to me words delivered by individuals that felt "off" and words that were given that felt "right." As I kept asking Him about these feelings, He first began to speak to me about the way I operated in His gifts. He said that I was operating from a polluted stream. He showed me a picture of two rivers merging into one. One river that flowed to me from my family was a prophetic stream that was pure, but there was another generational influence flowing to me out of my family's occult involvement in high-level Masonry. The Holy Spirit lovingly revealed to me that I was operating out of a muddied mixture of these two streams. I was "reading the souls of men", in essence, allowing psychic power or soul power to pollute the discernment that came from Him.

God began differentiating to me when I operated in the purity of the Holy Spirit's anointing and when I operated in my soul. When I was letting Holy Spirit bring the words, the focus of people was on God. When I was operating in my soul, the attention and glory came to me and my ability to be the helper or healer. God patiently dealt with me on this issue for several years. I still have to be intentional to focus my attention on the Holy Spirit when I am ministering prophetically. I am naturally intuitive, a blessing in the counseling room, but the various gifts of the Holy Spirit come from God, not intuition! God also showed me a similar unhealthy pattern in my life that was most obvious in how I used words of knowledge the Holy Spirit gave me. Basically, during the first 15 years of my ministry, the words of knowledge were mostly negative as in someone is having an affair, someone is sexually addicted, someone is holding a secret, etc. I would often know this information upon walking into a room of people. Then I would make an opportunity to pray over or have a conversation with that person, in essence I was manipulating them into telling me what was going on. (I was unaware of this wrong intention!) Next, I would pray for them or comfort them. In the end, the wonder of their relief was directed towards me, not the Father or the Holy Spirit.

As God uncovered this pattern, I was mortified as I saw the twisted ways that I had been operating. But my shame led to repentance and to learning a new way of ministering out of the gifts of the Holy Spirit. The reality is that we can, and probably all have ministered out of mixed motivations. What a blessing that the Holy Spirit is so faithful to convict and teach us a better way!

Another example of this pattern are the individuals I've met who tend to see an inordinate number of demonic things. I have come to understand that this "discernment" does not represent the Father's intention, which is light and freedom. I have watched the ministry of these people sometimes result in further oppression rather than being free. Jesus is a life-giver! This is another presentation of these folk's generational stream not being cleaned up fully.

Keep asking the Holy Spirit to reveal your impure motives and to clean up any muddy streams in your lives that are affecting how His gifts are used. He will be faithful to align us with His selfless flow!

Find a place in the Body of Christ where you can serve and be served.

When I moved to Kansas City, the Lord promised me that He would plant me in a new stream of His Body, that my church would bring me life and joy, and that I would bless them in return. This happened for a few years at my friends the O'Reilly's church, the Rock of KC. Long-term, God's fulfillment of His promise has come through our local church, Navah, a fellowship based in intimate communities within the larger Body which is affiliated with the 24/7 prayer network. Tim and I are positioned now as a mom and dad there, coaching and volunteer pastoring younger generations. We have the joy of hosting others in our home gatherings, and supporting in prayer the corporate gatherings. We are built up and encouraged in a Body. We need each other!

Recognize that seasons change. Ecclesiastes 3:1 says there is a season for everything under the sun.[56] Be patient in your waiting in every season.

I have had seasons where I was the banner builder and the dance choreographer and the prophetic expresser. I have had seasons of being a doer and producer and seasons of just being. I've had seasons of being out in front leading worship and seasons of hiddenness. There have been seasons of quietness and creativity and writing music, seasons where life brought me into constraint with homeschooling,

---

[56] *Amplified Holy Bible*, Ecclesiastes 3:1-8.

seasons where I was alone and seasons when I've had a partner, seasons when life require so much that I didn't have much to give others and seasons when I was constantly pouring out. There are many different seasons in our walk with Jesus. Sometimes He shares and talks a lot and at other times He is silent or very quiet. There are desert seasons and seasons of growth and maturing. The one constant is the Father of Lights Who doesn't change.

Tim and I are now living in the "latter will be greater than the former" season. We are experiencing restoration of marriage, of family, of a home, of a partnership of focus in our ministry. Tim, after moving to Kansas City from Los Angeles, founded and led a branch of the ministry of Joni and Friends.[57] We served this ministry together for two years with joy. Since retiring this past year, Tim is resting and volunteering, and he and I are merging and converging in ministry and loving it.

Tim sits in on my joint marriage sessions, we pray together over others, we help with strategic planning with the core leadership of our fellowship. His gift to bring order to things unites with my prophetic insight to form a powerful combined ministry. As we counsel young married couples, we often encourage them not only to affirm one another daily but to also really love their differences and laugh at their idiosyncrasies.

Tim and I are so very different, not just in gender but also in our approaches to life and counsel. Our combined approaches make for a balance that was not there when we were each alone. We've begun tag-teaming when we speak and it's so much fun and so well-rounded with each of our different perspectives!

In this season our families are slowly becoming friends with each of us. Tim has four grown children and I have four grown children. Each of us has three girls and a boy with the boy being third in the line-up. Even our kids' age spread is the same. How fun is that? We have 13 grandchildren at this time, but that's from only three of our kids! Three

---

[57] Joni and Friends International, Agoura Hills, CA

years into our marriage, our family is growing in both number and friendships with all of them.

Whatever season you are in --- chaotic or peaceful, quiet or intense, public or private --- God is with you and for you and He is shaping you into who you really are as His child. Remember and rest in His unchanging faithfulness as the One who restores and replenishes, and the One who gives us "everything pertaining to life and godliness".[58]Be content where He has you and let your circumstances produce the fruit God intended in you and through you. Even if we don't see the fullness of redemption here on earth, we have the confidence of all restoration occurring in eternity! This life isn't the real deal! Rest in the knowledge that He is the living God who endures forever.

For by Him all things were created in heaven and on earth, [things] visible and invisible, whether thrones or dominions or rulers or authorities; all things were created and exist through Him [that is, by His activity] and for Him. And He Himself existed and is before all things, and in Him all things hold together. [His is the controlling, cohesive force of the universe.] Colossians 1:16-17 Amplified Version

Father I ask that You would help me cultivate joy and thanksgiving in this season. If it feels like a dormant season, give me patience to wait for the Spring rain and for Your breath to blow new life. Help me trust You are at work in every aspect of what is going on or seemingly not going on. If it's one of great intensity, give me capacity for all You have put before me. If I'm unsure of what the next step is, lead my heart and mind into alignment with the path You have for me. Thank you for every good gift and for equipping me for everything I need to live a godly life before You. You know all things and You hold all things together, so I choose to trust and worship You.

---

[58] *New American Standard Bible*, 2 Peter 1:3.

Magnificent Lord
The One we adore
We stand in awe of Your grace
Perfection is Yours
Wonderful Lord
How can we not stand amazed!

Who is like You
Who is like You
What a wonder You are
Who is like You
Who is like You
No one else compares!

Higher, Your name is higher
You alone are God
Higher, Your name is higher
You alone are Lord

Laurie Goddu©

Made in the
USA
Monee, IL